Second Edition

GUIDE TO PARALLEL PROGRAMMING

On Sequent Computer Systems

Anita Osterhaug, Editor
Sequent Technical Publications

Prentice Hall, Englewood Cliffs, New Jersey 07632

Balance, DYNIX, and Practical Parallel are registered trademarks of Sequent Computer Systems, Inc. Symmetry is a trademark of Sequent Computer Systems, Inc.

UNIX is a registered trademark of AT&T.

MULTIBUS is a trademark of Intel Corporation.

Printed in the United States of America

10 9 8 7 6 5 4 3 2 1

ISBN 0-13-370446-7

Prentice-Hall International (UK) Limited, *London*
Prentice-Hall of Australia Pty. Limited, *Sydney*
Prentice-Hall Canada Inc., *Toronto*
Prentice-Hall Hispanoamericana, S.A., *Mexico*
Prentice-Hall of India Private Limited, *New Delhi*
Prentice-Hall of Japan, Inc., *Tokyo*
Simon & Schuster Asia Pte. Ltd., *Singapore*
Editora Prentice-Hall do Brasil, Ltda., *Rio de Janeiro*

Acknowledgements

The author wishes to thank all the people who contributed their time, expertise, and encouragement in the development of this book. In addition, many thanks to Sequent's "crg2" Symmetry computer, for its responsiveness and the faithful execution of its editing, formatting, and typesetting duties.

Cover design: Jeanne Galick

Cover photo: Dahlstrom Photography

About the cover: The cover is a graphic representation of a segment of the Mandelbrot set, the set of complex numbers which can be graphed as points on the complex plane. This image was generated by a Sequent B21 computer.

Table of Contents

About This Manual

Purpose

This manual introduces the basic concepts of parallel programming and explains how to develop parallel programs to run on a Sequent computer system.

Assumptions About the Reader

This manual assumes that you have experience writing, executing, and debugging C or FORTRAN programs. When developing your own parallel programs for a Sequent system, you should also have access to the other manuals in the Sequent software manual set, especially the *DYNIX Programmer's Manual*, which describes the standard commands, system calls, and subroutine libraries provided with the DYNIX operating system.

Overview of This Manual

This manual is organized as follows:

Chapter 1   **Parallel Programming and the Sequent System.** This chapter briefly introduces the Balance architecture and the two kinds of parallel programming: multiprogramming and multitasking.

Chapter 2   **Elements of Parallel Programming.** This chapter introduces terms and concepts that the user will need to be familiar with before designing a multitasking program and outlines two multitasking methods: data partitioning and function partitioning.

Chapter 3   **Parallel Programming Tools.** This chapter describes some of the parallel programming tools that have been implemented on Sequent systems.

Chapter 4   **Data Partitioning with Sequent FORTRAN.** This chapter explains how to use the FORTRAN parallel programming directives to execute DO loop iterations in parallel.

In addition to the contents listed above, this manual contains an index to aid you in locating information and a glossary of parallel programming terms.

Chapter 1

Parallel Programming and the Sequent System

Chapter 1

Parallel Programming and the Sequent System

1.1. Introduction

This chapter introduces the Sequent system architecture and discusses the parallel programming capabilities of the system.

1.2. Sequent Systems

Sequent systems are true *multiprocessors*, computers that incorporate multiple identical processors (CPUs) and a single common memory. The Sequent CPUs are general-purpose, 32-bit microprocessors. The following characteristics distinguish the Sequent architecture from other parallel architectures:

- **True multiprocessor.** Sequent systems are true multiprocessors, not array processors or ensemble machines.

- **Tightly coupled.** All processors share a single pool of memory, to enhance resource sharing and communication among different processes.

- **Common bus.** All processors, memory modules, and I/O controllers plug into a single high-speed bus, making it simple to add processors, memory, and I/O bandwidth.

- **Symmetric.** All processors are identical, and all processors can execute both user code and kernel (operating system) code.

- **Transparent.** Programs written for a single-processor system can run on a Sequent system without modifications for multiprocessing support. Processors can be added or removed without modifying the operating system or user applications.

- **Dynamic load balancing.** Processors automatically schedule themselves to ensure that all processors are kept busy as long as there are executable processes (instruction streams) available. When a processor stops executing one process (e.g., because that process is finished or is waiting for an I/O operation), it begins executing the next available process in the system-wide run queue.

- **Shared memory.** An application can consist of multiple processes, all accessing shared data structures in memory.

- **Hardware support for mutual exclusion.** To support exclusive access to shared data structures, the system allows the user to lock any section of physical memory.

Sequent offers two product lines: the Balance Series and the Symmetry Series. The Balance Series supports parallel programming and research as well as a wide variety of commercial applications. The Symmetry Series offers higher performance and larger memory configurations at a slightly higher price.

The Balance Series includes the Sequent B8 and B21 systems. The smaller system, the Sequent B8, can include from 2 to 12 processors. The larger system, the Sequent B21, can include from 4 to 30 processors. Balance systems can be configured with 4 to 28 Mbytes of memory, and they provide 16 Mbytes of virtual address space per process. In Balance systems, each CPU has 8 Kbytes of cache RAM. (The cache RAM greatly reduces the number of times each processor must access system memory.)

The Symmetry Series includes the Sequent S27 and S81 systems. The Sequent S27 can include from 2 to 10 processors, while the Sequent S81 can include from 2 to 30 processors. Symmetry systems can also include one floating-point accelerator per processor. Symmetry systems can be configured with 8 to 240 Mbytes of memory, and they provide 256 Mbytes of virtual address space per process. In Symmetry systems, each CPU has 64 Kbytes of cache RAM.

For secondary mass storage, Sequent systems offer both disk and tape drives. Sequent systems are available with 5 ¼-inch, 8-inch, or 10-inch disks and can be configured with up to 32 disks of any one type. In addition, the systems can contain up to four reel-to-reel tape drives. Both 6250-bpi and 1600-bpi drives are available.

Sequent computers run the DYNIX operating system, a version of UNIX 4.2bsd that also supports most utilities, libraries, and system calls provided by UNIX System V. A fully-configured Sequent system can support up to 256 users.

1.3. Parallel Programming

Sequent systems support the two basic kinds of parallel programming: multiprogramming and multitasking. *Multiprogramming* is an operating system feature that allows a computer to execute multiple unrelated programs concurrently. (A multi-user operating system is a good example of this.) *Multitasking* is a programming technique that allows a single application to consist of multiple processes executing concurrently. This manual is primarily about multitasking, since the DYNIX operating system does multiprogramming for all user programs automatically.

Many systems offer multiprogramming and some offer multitasking, but a Sequent system offers these features with an important difference. By definition, parallel programs execute *concurrently*, meaning that at any instant, the system is in the process of executing multiple programs. On a Sequent system, parallel programs execute *simultaneously*: at any instant, the system can be executing multiple instructions from multiple processes. Thus, parallel programming on a Sequent system has two special benefits: multiprogramming yields improved *system throughput* for multiple programs, and multitasking yields improved *execution speed* for individual programs.

1.3.1 Multiprogramming on a Sequent System

The multi-user, multiprogrammed UNIX environment adapts quite naturally to the Sequent multiprocessing architecture and automatically schedules processes for optimal throughput. In other versions of the UNIX operating system, executable processes wait in a run queue; when the CPU suspends or terminates execution of one process, it switches to the process at the head of the run queue. DYNIX uses the same technique, except that a pool of processors is available to execute processes from the run queue. DYNIX balances the system load among the available processors, keeping all processors busy as long as there is enough work available, thus using the full computing capability of each processor.

On a Sequent system, workloads consisting of multiple, single-stream, compute-intensive applications show a nearly linear increase in system throughput as more processors are added. Even applications that require significant amounts of I/O activity, such as document formatters and compilers, show performance-per-processor curves well above those previously thought possible, and this increase in performance is achieved with no extra effort by the programmer.

1.3.2 Multitasking on a Sequent System

The Sequent system supports multitasking by allowing a single application to consist of multiple, closely cooperating processes. In fact, the
DYNIX operating system automatically does multitasking for some
applications: the **Make** utility automatically executes software build
operations in parallel, and the **lint** utility does parallel consistency checking on C program modules. The DYNIX **sh** and **apply** utilities allow you
to create parallel processes or execute system commands in parallel.

The Sequent language software includes multitasking extensions to C,
Pascal, and FORTRAN. The DYNIX Parallel Programming Library
includes routines to create, synchronize, and terminate parallel processes
from C, Pascal, and FORTRAN programs.

The speedup that can be gained by multitasking is determined by the following factors:

- The percent of the program's time that can be spent executing
  parallel code. This factor varies with the application, but a
  surprisingly large variety of applications need to spend less than
  1% of their time executing sequential code.

- The number of processors available to the application (see Section 1.2). The Sequent software allows you to design programs
  that adapt themselves to the number of processors in the system, so that the same program can run on different-sized systems without modification.

- The hardware contention imposed by multiple processors com-
  peting for the same resources, such as the system bus and system memory. On Sequent systems, this overhead is negligible,
  since most CPU memory operations access cache memory, not
  the system bus.

- The overhead in creating multiple processes. This overhead is
  measured in only hundredths of a second per process.

- The overhead in synchronization and communication among
  multiple processes. Because the Sequent architecture includes
  shared memory and hardware-based synchronization facilities,
  this overhead is measured in microseconds.

The remainder of this manual explains in detail how to develop efficient
multitasking programs on the Sequent system. Chapter 2 discusses
parallel programming terms and concepts. Chapter 3 discusses several

parallel programming models that have been implemented on Sequent systems. Chapters 4 through 6 explain how to create parallel programs using Sequent multitasking tools.

Chapter 2

Elements of Parallel Programming

Chapter 2

Elements of Parallel Programming

2.1. Introduction

This chapter introduces some principles of parallel programming and some terms and concepts that you will need to know before designing a parallel program. Section 2.2 explains the goals of a parallel programmer and takes you through the process of identifying the parallelism in an example job. Section 2.3 describes the two basic multitasking methods: *data partitioning* and *function partitioning*. The remaining sections introduce some elements of parallel programming that are not common in sequential programming, including:

- Creation and termination of multiple processes

- Creation of shared and private data

- *Scheduling*, the division of computing tasks among parallel processes

- Interprocess communication

- Task synchronization and mutual exclusion

- I/O from parallel processes

2.2. Programming Goals

In adapting an application for multitasking, you will have the following goals:

- Run as much of the program in parallel as possible.

- Balance the computational load as evenly as possible among parallel processes.

The extent to which you meet these goals ultimately determines the execution speed of the program.

To help illustrate the importance of these goals, imagine an automobile repair shop with four equally skilled repairpeople, Joe, Gary, Dave, and Sue. If Joe can change the tires on a car in two hours, the four repairpeople should be able to change the four tires in a half hour, right? Not necessarily. Let's look at the tasks involved in changing a tire:

1. Fill out the paperwork while the customer describes the work to be done. **(10 minutes)**

2. Get the new tires out of stock. **(10 minutes or 5 minutes/pair)**

3. Drive the car into the shop and raise it on a hydraulic lift. **(10 minutes)**

4. Change the four tires. **(15 minutes/tire)**

5. Lower the hydraulic lift and drive the car out of the garage. **(10 minutes)**

6. Discard the old tires. **(10 minutes or 5 minutes/pair)**

7. Prepare the bill and charge the customer. **(10 minutes)**

Clearly, the four repair people could change the tires at the same time, leaving the paperwork and miscellaneous jobs to Joe. If we chart the shop activities based on this assumption, the job takes 1 hour and 15 minutes, as illustrated in Figure 2-1.

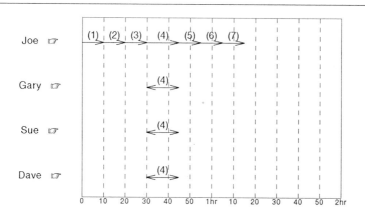

Fig. 2-1. Changing tires: parallel approach.

Notice, however, that with this approach, three of the repair people are doing nothing for an hour each: the workload is not well-balanced. There are three person-hours of idle time and the job is completed only 45 minutes sooner than when Joe does the whole job himself.

Let's try another approach and see if we can better meet the multitasking goals: to balance the workload and do as much of the job in parallel as possible. Maybe we can shorten the job and eliminate some waste by having Gary, Dave, and Sue handle more tasks in parallel with Joe.

Let's say that after talking with the customer for five minutes, Joe knows what kind of tires the customer wants. He could send both Gary and Sue to get a pair of tires while he completes arrangements with the customer. Dave is still idle, so Joe could send Dave to put the car on the hydraulic lift. (Naturally, Joe has to take a little time to explain what he wants the others to do, but for now let's assume that the time is negligible.) At this point, Joe finishes the paperwork and Gary and Sue arrive with the new tires. However, Dave is still putting the car on the lift. Joe, Gary, and Sue must wait for Dave. Here the job has an inherent *order dependency*, a point where a task depends on the result of a previous task and cannot proceed until the previous task is finished. (Section 2.7 explains more about dependences.)

Once the car is on the lift, the four repair people can change the tires in parallel. After the tires are changed, Joe can finish the paperwork and charge the customer. At the same time, Gary and Sue can discard the old tires and Dave can lower the car and drive it out of the shop. Figure 2-2 illustrates this task sequence.

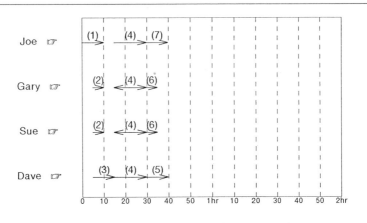

Fig. 2-2. Changing tires: balanced parallel approach.

The repair people are now doing as many tasks in parallel as the job allows, and the workload is distributed as evenly as possible. The total job takes only 40 minutes. (Notice that this is very close to the original guess; that is, that four people could do the job in 30 minutes.) The repair people collectively have only 40 minutes of idle time, and this task sequence is 1 hour and 20 minutes faster than when Joe did the whole job himself.

Adapting an application for multitasking is very much like scheduling work in Joe's auto shop. Virtually every application has certain inherent dependences that prohibit completely parallel execution. However, you can achieve the shortest possible execution time by executing as many tasks in parallel as possible and by balancing the workload. In a surprising number of applications, you will find that 99% of the computation required can be done in parallel.

2.3. Programming Methods: Data and Function Partitioning

The first step in adapting an application for efficient multitasking is to choose the right programming method. Most applications naturally lend themselves to one of two multitasking programming methods: *data partitioning* or *function partitioning*.

Data partitioning involves creating multiple, identical processes and assigning a portion of the data to each process. (This method is sometimes called *homogeneous multitasking*, because it involves identical tasks executed in parallel.) Data partitioning is appropriate for applications that perform the same operations repeatedly on large collections of data. In the auto shop example, fetching tires in parallel and changing tires in parallel are examples of data partitioning. In programming terms, data partitioning is appropriate for applications that require loops to perform calculations on arrays or matrices: data partitioning is done by executing the loop iterations in parallel. Algorithms such as matrix multiplication or Fourier transformations and applications such as ray tracing or signal processing adapt well to data partitioning.

Function partitioning, on the other hand, involves creating multiple unique processes and having them simultaneously perform different operations on a shared data set. (This method is sometimes called *heterogeneous multitasking*, because it involves different tasks executed in parallel.) Function partitioning is suitable for applications which must perform many different operations on the same data. In programming terms, function partitioning is appropriate for applications that include many unique subroutines or functions. Applications such as flight simulation, program compilation, and traditional process control adapt well to function partitioning.

While some applications require function partitioning, and some applications lend themselves to a combination of these methods, most applications adapt most easily to data partitioning. While both programming methods can be effective, the data partitioning method offers the following advantages over function partitioning:

- Workloads are easy to balance among processors.

- Minimal programming effort is required.

- Programs adapt automatically to the number of processors in a system.

2.4. Process Creation and Termination

Process creation is analagous to hiring repair people for Joe's garage, and similar considerations apply. Joe needs enough employees to get work done quickly, but he has to pay them even when there is no work for them to do. Therefore, Joe wants only as many employees as he can keep busy most of the time. A parallel programmer has to make the same tradeoffs, only instead of employees the programmer has UNIX processes. The programmer needs enough processes to execute a program quickly, but not so many that they are often sitting idle and consuming CPU cycles, waiting for work.

In DYNIX, as in other UNIX-based operating systems, a new process is created by using a system call called a *fork*. The new (or *child*) process is a duplicate copy of the old (or *parent*) process, with the same data, register contents, and program counter. If the parent has files open or has access to shared memory, the child has access to the same files and shared memory. So that the parent and child know which process is which, a *process identification number* or process ID is returned to each. When a child process is created, the process ID number 0 is returned to the child, and the child's process ID number is returned to the parent. From this point on, the parent and child are separate entities.

A UNIX fork operation is relatively expensive. Therefore, a parallel application typically forks as many processes as it is likely to need at the beginning of the program, and does not terminate any process until the program is complete. If a process is not needed during certain code sequences, the process can wait in a busy loop or relinquish the processor until it is needed. (The cost to an existing process of relinquishing a processor and later reacquiring it is rather low, while the cost of spinning can be very high in terms of system throughput.)

2.5. Shared and Private Data

Typically, multitasking programs include both shared and private data. Shared data is accessible by both parent and child processes. Private data is accessible by only one process. In the "Joe's garage" example, the car might be considered shared data, since it was accessible to all the repair people, and the tires might be considered private data, because each repair person had his or her own tire to work with.

There are several advantages to sharing data:

- It uses less memory than having multiple copies.

- It avoids the overhead of making copies of the data for each process.

- Most important, it provides a simple and efficient mechanism for communication between processes. (Section 3.5 discusses this communication.)

On a Balance system, each process has 16 Mbytes of virtual memory; on a Symmetry system, each process has 256 Mbytes. This memory space contains the process's *text* (program source) area, its private data area, and its private stack. A program may expand its private data area using a system call such as `brk()` or a routine such as `malloc()`. The portion of the data area that is allocated at run time is called the *heap*. If the program includes any shared data, the process's virtual memory space also contains a shared data area and a shared heap. If the program calls routines in the DYNIX Parallel Programming Library, it may also contain a shared stack. Figure 2-3 illustrates the virtual memory contents of a process.

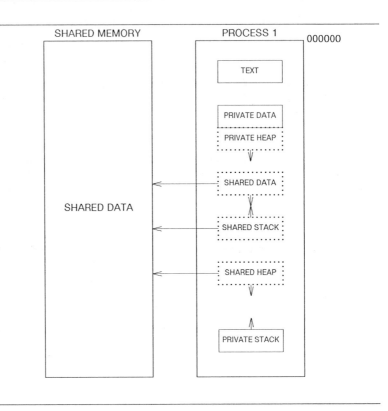

Fig. 2-3. Process virtual memory contents.

Notice that as memory is allocated, the heaps grow from lower memory addresses to higher ones, while the stacks grow in the opposite direction. An integer variable named _stack_limit determines how large the stacks can grow. In the case of the shared heap and the private stack, the variable acts as both an upper bound for the stack and a lower bound for the heap. The DYNIX **limit** command displays the default value of _stack_limit. You can assign new values within your parallel programs.

If the process forks any child processes, each child process inherits access to the parent's shared memory area and shared stack. Both the parent and children can then access the shared data.

The Sequent FORTRAN, C, and Pascal compilers all include mechanisms to designate data as shared or private. Chapters 4, 5, and 6 explain how to use these mechanisms to create shared and private data for data partitioning and function partitioning applications.

2.6. Scheduling Algorithms

In multitasking programs, tasks can be scheduled among processes using three types of algorithms: prescheduling, static scheduling, or dynamic scheduling.

In prescheduling, the task division is determined by the programmer before the program is compiled. Prescheduled programs cannot automatically balance the computing load according to the data or the number of CPUs in the system. Therefore, this method is appropriate only for function partitioning applications, where each process is performing a different task. To schedule, the programmer assigns a specific task to each processor. For example, one processor may be responsible for handling signals from input devices, and another processor may be responsible for updating a graphics frame buffer.

In static scheduling, the tasks are scheduled by the processes at run time, but they are divided in some predetermined way. The static scheduling algorithm for a process is:

1. Figure out which tasks I will do.

2. Do all my tasks.

3. Wait until all other processes finish their tasks.

For example, your program might include a 100-iteration loop. Using static scheduling, if your program uses 10 processes, each process might execute 10 iterations of the loop.

In dynamic scheduling, each process schedules its own tasks at run time by checking a task queue or a "do-me-next" array index. The scheduling algorithm for a process is:

1. Wait until some tasks appear.

2. Remove the first task from the list and do it.

3. If there are any more tasks, go to step 2. Otherwise, go to step 1.

For example, a dynamically scheduled program might perform a matrix multiply, with each process computing three matrix elements and then returning for more until all the work is done.

Dynamic scheduling provides dynamic load balancing: all processes keep working as long as there is work to be done. Since the workload is evenly distributed among the processes, the work can be completed sooner. Static scheduling produces static load balancing: since the division of tasks is statically determined, several processors may stand idle while one processor completes its share of the job. However, dynamic scheduling entails more overhead than static scheduling. Each time a process schedules another task for itself, it must check the shared queue to make sure there is work to do, and it must remove that task from the queue. Generally, unless each task is to work on a very small amount of data each time it schedules a chunk of work, or you know in advance that static scheduling is efficient for your application, it is best to use dynamic scheduling.

Static and dynamic scheduling are most easily achieved with homogeneous multitasking algorithms. However, dynamic scheduling is also possible with heterogeneous tasks, as evidenced by the DYNIX operating system itself.

2.7. Program Dependence

Program dependence is a formal theory which defines how, in order to guarantee correct results, some program operations *depend* on previous operations, while some may be executed in any order. When you have defined the full set of program dependences for any program unit, you have identified all the ordering necessary to guarantee correct results. There are two classes of program dependence: *data dependence* and *control dependence*. This section presents a brief introduction to program dependence.

When a program unit has no dependences, the statements can be executed in any order, including simultaneously. In the following example, statements 2 and 3 are completely independent and can be executed in any order:

```
1    A = B + C
2    D = A * 5
3    E = A + 6
```

There are three types of data dependence. The first and most familiar is called *flow dependence* or *true dependence*. It occurs when one operation sets a data value that is used by ("flows to") a subsequent operation. In the above example, the value A is set in statement 1 and used in statement 2. Statement 3 also depends on statement 1.

The second type of data dependence, an *antidependence* occurs when one operation uses a memory location that is loaded by a subsequent operation. In the following example, statement 1 must execute before statement 2, since statement 1 uses the current value of C. This kind of dependence is a consideration when executing loops in parallel.

```
1    A = B + C
2    C = B * 5.
3    A = D - 6.
```

The final type of data dependence, *output dependence*, occurs when one operation loads a memory location which is also loaded in a subsequent operation. In the above example statement 3 must execute after statement 1, or A will contain the wrong data value at the end of this program segment.

The other category of program dependence is called *control dependence*. This category includes dependences that are due to the required flow of control in a program. In the following example, statement 2 is conditionally executed depending on the results of the test in statement 1.

```
1    IF ( X .GT. 0 )
2       A = B + 5.
```

If you can identify all the program dependences within a program unit, you can determine the set of synchronization points and mechanisms required to transform a given program, loop, or subroutine to correctly run in parallel. Process synchronization is discussed in the following section, and some special mechanisms for use in parallelizing FORTRAN loops are discussed in Chapter 4. Appendix C describes code optimizations which can minimize the number of synchronizations required, thus raising the percentage of code that can execute in parallel while preserving the correctness of the code.

The examples given here are all straight-line, statement-level FORTRAN code, but it should be obvious that the principles described can be extended to other languages, looping code segments, and different program units such as subroutines or procedures. It should also be clear that these program dependences can be discovered and transformed manually, or by an automatic translator, or both. Chapter 4 gives detailed instructions for manually identifying the dependences needed to correctly parallelize a large percentage of FORTRAN loops.

In the future, there will be increasing emphasis on the use of automatic parallelizing tools (which will operate in conjunction with the invaluable assistance which a programmer can supply). For now it is sufficient to recognize that all real application programs contain program dependences, and that synchronization mechanisms can be used to ensure correct parallel execution of these programs.

NOTE

The theory of data dependence was pioneered by Kuck and associates at the University of Illinois and is concisely described in a recent paper by Padua and Wolfe[1].

2.8. Process Synchronization

We define a semaphore as a shared data structure used to synchronize the actions of multiple cooperating processes. The simplest type of semaphore in a Sequent system (and the semaphore upon which all others can be based) is a lock (also called a spinlock).

2.8.1 Locks

A lock ensures that only one process at a time can access a shared data structure. A lock has two values: locked and unlocked. Before attempting to access a shared data structure, a process waits until the lock associated with the data structure is unlocked, indicating that no other process is accessing the data structure. The process then locks the lock, accesses the data structure, and unlocks the lock. While a process is waiting for a lock to become unlocked, it spins in a tight loop, producing no work — hence the name "spinlock." This spinning is also referred to as a *busy wait*.

The locking mechanisms provided on Sequent systems perform the actions required to acquire a lock (see that it is unlocked; then relock it) as a single indivisible operation. Hence it is impossible for two processes to acquire a lock at the same time, and the locking operations are very fast because there is no operating system intervention.

---

1. Padua, D.A. and M.J. Wolfe. "Advanced Compiler Optimization for Supercomputers." *Communications of the ACM* Vol. 29, No. 12, December 1986, pp. 1184-1201.

A critical code section begins with a lock operation and ends with an unlock operation. Figure 2-4 illustrates how a lock is used to prevent multiple processes from executing a dependent section simultaneously.

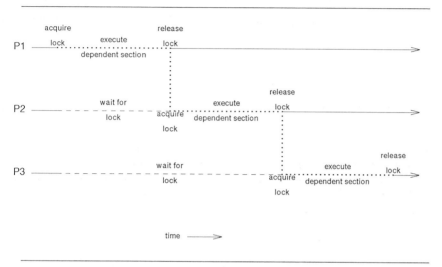

Fig. 2-4. Role of lock in protecting dependent section.
This figure illustrates what happens when three processors all try to enter a dependent section simultaneously. All processors attempt to acquire the lock immediately, but only P1 succeeds: P2 and P3 must wait while P1 executes the dependent section. When P1 releases the lock, P2 and P3 again attempt to acquire it, and P2 wins: P3 must wait again.

2.8.2 Ordering and Counting/Queuing Semaphores

Semaphores other than locks can be used to protect order-dependent sections and manage queues.

Ordering Semaphores

Ordering semaphores are used to ensure that order-dependent code sections are executed in the proper order. To do this, you create a semaphore, N, to indicate how many times the dependent section has been executed. The algorithm for a process using the semaphore is:

1. Figure out which iteration of the dependent section to execute next.

2. If N equals the iteration number, execute the dependent section.

3. If N does not equal the iteration number, spin until it does and then execute the dependent section.

4. After executing the dependent section, increment N.

Counting/queuing Semaphores

Counting/queuing semaphores are useful for queue management. When several processes are waiting for a lock, the lock will go to the first process that tries to acquire it after it is unlocked. Counting/queuing semaphores can ensure that the lock is assigned instead to the process that has waited the longest for it. This type of semaphore is also useful for managing several instances of a given resource (such as message buffers). In these situations, the value N of a counting/queuing semaphore can be interpreted as follows:

N>0	N is the number of instances of the resource available. When the semaphore guards a single data structure, $N=1$ means the semaphore is unlocked.
N≤0	No instances of the resource are available (or the semaphore is locked). $-N$ is the number of processors waiting for the resource to become available.

The algorithm for acquiring (locking) such a semaphore is:

1. Decrement the semaphore value, N.

2. If N is less than 0, put my process ID in the $-N$th slot of the queue of waiting processes, and wait for someone to tell me it's my turn.

The algorithm for releasing the semaphore is:

1. If N is less than 0, notify the process at the head of the queue that it's his turn, and adjust the queue accordingly.

2. Increment N.

Note that all accesses to the semaphore value and wait queue must be protected by spinlocks.

The `semop()` system call, which has been incorporated into DYNIX from UNIX System V, is a widely used mechanism for implementing a more general version of counting/queuing semaphores. However, `semop()` does not guarantee that the first process in the queue will be the next to acquire the semaphore.

Spin or Block?

An important consideration that affects how you use semaphores is what a process should do while it is waiting. Four possibilities are:

- Don't wait. Go do something else and check the semaphore later.

- Spin (busy wait). This minimizes overhead, but spinning for long periods of time (for example, during I/O operations) wastes processor cycles.

- Spin for a specified period of time (or number of loops), then block.

- Block (relinquish the processor to another job). Under certain circumstances, this may be the only acceptable course of action during potentially long waits. On the other hand, if your job needs to run at top priority with a minimum of overhead, you may choose to forego this courtesy at the expense of system throughput.

For example, a process that uses the `semop()` system call will block until the requested semaphore is available. A process that uses the `s_lock` or `m_lock` routine from the DYNIX Parallel Programming Library will spin until the requested lock is available.

2.8.3 Events

An *event* is something that must happen before a task or process can proceed. Examples of events are:

- completion of a task

- appearance of a task in a formerly empty task queue

- arrival of needed data

- arrival of the last process at a synchronization point

Events have two values: posted and cleared. One or more processes *wait* for an event until another process *posts* the event. The waiting processes then proceed. The event may need to be *cleared* by the waiting process, by a master process, or by another process, depending on the program.

2.8.4 Barriers

A *barrier* is a synchronization point. The code executed at a barrier is usually something like this:

1. Mark myself as present at the barrier.

2. Wait for all the other processes to arrive.

3. Proceed.

The determination that all processes are present at the barrier may be made by the last process to arrive, by a master process, or by all processes independently.

2.9. I/O

I/O in parallel programs is complicated by two factors:

- The need for caution when multiple processes write to the same file

- The tendency for a process to block (relinquish its processor) during an I/O operation

These complications can usually be reduced by performing I/O only during sequential phases of the program or by designating one process as a server to perform all I/O. Refer to Appendix A, "Factors Affecting Performance," for more information on this topic.

Chapter 3

Parallel Programming Tools

Chapter 3

Parallel Programming Tools

3.1. Introduction

This chapter describes some of the programming tools available on Sequent systems. Some of these tools are available from Sequent and some have been developed by Sequent users. Together, they show the wide range of parallel programming approaches that are supported by Sequent systems.

The applications that can be adapted for parallel programming vary greatly in their requirements for data sharing, interprocess communication, and synchronization. To gain optimal speed-up from a parallel solution, the programmer must develop an algorithm that meets the requirements of the application while still exploiting all of its inherent parallelism. To aid in this effort, the programmer needs tools that adapt easily to the needs of a given application.

For example, a matrix multiplication on a large data set is best expressed in terms of data partitioning: the solution requires repeating the same operation on many different data items. This problem is very synchronous. The program will have a well-defined beginning and end, and the programmer can easily predict at what points the processes must synchronize or communicate shared data. Ideal tools for this application would support creation and termination of multiple identical processes and division of shared data among processes.

In contrast, a large data base application might be much better expressed in terms of function partitioning. At any time, different users may be using different utilities to access the data base. These processes may need to communicate to share data, or one process may need to ensure that another process doesn't corrupt its data. This application is asynchronous: the programmer cannot predict when users will create processes that need to communicate or access shared data. This application requires tools that allow processes to communicate on an as-needed basis.

The Sequent systems support programming tools for a wide range of applications:

- The FORTRAN parallel programming directives support parallel execution of FORTRAN DO loops. With these directives, users can execute many DO loops in parallel simply by adding a single line to the source code.

- The microtasking routines in the Parallel Programming Library support data and function partitioning applications. They allow users to quickly and easily create sets of processes, schedule tasks among processes, and synchronize processes between tasks.

- The Force is a flexible tool which adapts to both data partitioning and function partitioning applications. In addition to the process creation, scheduling, and synchronization capabilities of data partitioning tools, it supports synchronization based on availability of shared data.

- The DYNIX operating system includes a number of facilities that support communication of data and status information between loosely related processes.

- The parallel Ada tasking facility supports a similarly asynchronous programming approach.

The following sections briefly describe these tools.

3.2. FORTRAN Parallel Programming Directives

The Sequent FORTRAN compiler can restructure DO loops for parallel execution. The user prepares the program for the preprocessor by inserting a set of directives which identify the loops to be executed in parallel, the shared and private data within each loop, and any critical sections of the loops (loop sections containing dependences). The directives also allow the user to control the scheduling of loop iterations among processes and the division of data between processes. The directive are described in the *Sequent FORTRAN Compiler User's Guide*.

Once the user has identified the parallel loops and properly marked the data and critical sections, the preprocessor handles all the low-level tasks of data partitioning. The preprocessor produces a program that transparently sets up shared data structures, creates a set of identical processes, schedules tasks among processes, and handles mutual exclusion and process synchronization.

Chapter 4 explains how to use the FORTRAN parallel programming directives and how to analyze DO loops to identify shared and private data and critical code sections.

3.3. Parallel Programming Library

The Sequent Parallel Programming Library is a set of C routines which allow the programmer to execute C, FORTRAN, or Pascal subprograms in parallel. The library includes routines to handle the following functions:

- Allocation of memory for shared data

- Creation of processes to execute subprograms in parallel

- Identification of individual processes

- Suspension of processes during serial program sections

- Mutual exclusion on shared data

- Synchronization of processes during critical sections

Programs that use the Parallel Programming Library can be made to automatically balance loads between processors and to automatically adjust the division of computing tasks at run time based on the number of processors configured in the system. The library routines allow the programmer to handle the communication and synchronization needs of an algorithm at a high level while concentrating on the design of the parallel algorithm.

Chapter 5 explains how to use the Parallel Programming Library and illustrates some data analysis and scheduling techniques.

3.4. The Force

The Force is a set of FORTRAN macros developed by Harry Jordan of the University of Colorado at Boulder. These macros support standard data partitioning in a manner similar to the Sequent FORTRAN parallel programming directives, but they also offer support for less synchronous solutions.

For simple data partitioning, the Force provides automatic process creation and termination, declaration of shared and private data, and synchronization of critical code sections. It will restructure loops for parallel execution using either prescheduling or self-scheduling.

The Force also includes a special data type, Async, and two special operations, Produce and Consume, that allow synchronization based on data availability. An Async variable is a shared variable that has a "full/empty" state flag associated with it. An Async variable is marked full by a Produce operation. If the variable is already full, the Produce operation waits until the variable is empty before writing a new value. When a process performs a Consume operation on an Async variable, the Force verifies that the Async variable is in the full state. If not, the Consume operation waits until the variable is full, executes, and then sets the variable state to empty.

For more information about the Force and where to obtain the Force macros for Sequent computers, contact Sequent Technical Marketing.

3.5. UNIX Function Partitioning Tools

The DYNIX operating system provides support for asynchronous parallel programming through standard UNIX 4.2bsd system calls, with special DYNIX system calls and libraries, and with system calls in the System V Applications Environment (SVAE).

UNIX system calls such as `sigpause()`, `sigvec()`, and `sigblock()` allow processes to send and receive signals among themselves. The SVAE system calls `semop()`, `semget()`, and `semctl()` allow programs to create and use counting and blocking semaphores. The UNIX Interprocess Communication (IPC) subsystem allows processes to perform direct data transfers among themselves, even across a network of systems. The SVAE message-passing system calls allow processes to send and receive data via message queues. Together, these facilities support a wide range of function partitioning applications, ranging from a single program with a set of unique parallel processes to a set of programs working on a shared data base.

All of these facilities are described in more detail in Chapter 5.

3.6. Parallel Ada

The standard Ada language supports an asynchronous approach to parallel programming. The Ada language includes program structures called *tasks*. Tasks resemble subroutines except that, by definition, they can be executed in parallel. The Sequent Parallel Run-Time System (PRTS) allows Ada tasks to execute in parallel.

Ada tasks communicate and synchronize with each other through ENTRY, ACCEPT, and "call" statements. A task can include several ENTRY declarations, each of which represents a subroutine declaration. The task's ENTRY declarations and the corresponding ACCEPT statements in the task body define all the operations that a task of that type can perform when it is called by another task. A call statement resembles a function call that specifies the task being called, the desired ENTRY in the called task, and the arguments to be passed to the called task.

At any time during program execution, one task can call another. It then suspends its execution until the called task executes the corresponding ACCEPT statement. Once the ACCEPT statement is present, the two tasks are said to be "in rendezvous". At this point, the calling task is suspended until the accepting task has completed the operations for that ENTRY and passed the results back. Both tasks can then resume parallel execution until either needs to rendezvous with another task.

For more information on the Sequent PRTS, contact Sequent Marketing.

3.7. Other Tools

Parallel researchers have implemented a variety of other parallel programming tools on Sequent machines. Herb Schwetman of MCC has developed PPL©, a C-based parallel programming language with built-in process management features. (Appendix D gives a reference for a paper on PPL.) Several Sequent users have developed hypercube simulators for use on their Sequent systems. Dr. Eugene Brooks of Lawrence Livermore National Laboratories has implemented gang scheduling of processes on a Sequent system.

Most applications can be solved efficiently with parallel programming. The programming tools described in this chapter can be applied to a wide range of applications, and parallel programmers are constantly developing new tools that can be run on Sequent systems. With its symmetric architecture, shared memory, and built-in parallel programming support, the Sequent architecture can support almost any application and parallel programming model.

Chapter 4

Data Partitioning with Sequent FORTRAN

Page

Tables

Illustrations

Chapter 4

Data Partitioning with Sequent FORTRAN

4.1. Introduction

This chapter explains how to convert FORTRAN DO loops for data partitioning. Sequent FORTRAN includes a set of special directives for parallel loops. With these directives, you mark the loop to be executed in parallel and classify loop variables so that data is passed correctly between loop iterations. The FORTRAN compiler interprets the directives and restructures the source code for data partitioning.

There are three criteria you should use when selecting a loop for parallel execution:

- If possible, choose the outermost loop in a program or program section.

- Always choose a loop which accounts for a large portion of the computation done by the program.

- Whenever possible, choose an independent loop.

You can use the DYNIX *gprof* utility to determine which loops are responsible for the most computation. Refer to Appendix B for more information on *gprof*.

Ideally, the loops you choose for parallel execution should be independent loops, loops in which no iteration depends the operations in any other iteration. You can determine whether a loop is independent by answering the following question: "If this loop were executed one iteration at a time but in random order, would it still produce correct results?" If the answer is yes, the loop is independent; if not, then the loop is dependent. If you determine that a loop is dependent, but the dependences account for only a small portion of the processing done by the loop, there is still an advantage to executing the loop in parallel. You may even be able to minimize the dependences by moving the statements that carry dependences closer together.

The remainder of this chapter is organized as follows:

- Section 4.2 explains how to analyze data flow within a DO loop and how to use the parallel programming directives to prepare the loop for parallel execution.

- Section 4.3 explains briefly how to compile, load, execute, and debug your program.

- Section 4.4 lists additional sources of information.

4.2. Preparing DO Loops

To prepare a DO loop for parallel execution, follow these steps:

1. Analyze the variables in the loop and classify them according to usage. (Section 4.2.1 explains how to analyze variable usage.)

   NOTE

   > *The loop index is not considered to be a variable within the loop. There is no need to analyze its usage. Other variables appearing in the loop control statement do not need to be analyzed unless they also appear within the body of the loop.*

2. Use the parallel programming directives to identify the loop to be executed in parallel and to specify the variable types. (Section 4.2.2 explains how to use the parallel programming directives.)

3. If necessary, call DYNIX Parallel Programming Library routines to preserve correct data flow within the loop. (Section 4.2.2 explains when and how to use the Parallel Programming Library in DO loops.)

4.2.1 Analyzing Variable Usage

The first step in preparing a FORTRAN DO loop for data partitioning is to analyze how each variable in the loop is used. You have already done some of this: when you determined which loop to execute in parallel, you had to analyze variable usage in order to determine which loops were independent. Now you need to examine and classify each variable in the loop into one of the following categories:

- Shared variables

- Local variables

- Reduction variables

- Shared ordered variables

- Shared locked variables

The remainder of this section explains how to identify each type of variable and presents a worksheet to aid you in classifying the variables in your program.

Shared Variables

A shared variable is an array or scalar (single-element) variable that has one of the following properties:

- It is *read-only*; that is, it is never assigned a value within the loop.

- It is an array and each element is referenced by only one loop iteration. (This occurs when the array index varies directly with the loop index.)

In the following example loop, all the variables are shared:

```
      DO 1 k = 1,n
   1        X(k) = Q + Y(k)*(R*Z(k+10) + T*Z(k+11))
```

The variables Q, Y, R, z, and T meet the first test for a shared variable: they are never assigned values within the loop. The only variable that appears on the left side of an assignment statement is x, which meets the second test for a shared variable: it is an array and each element is read and written by only one iteration. (We can tell because its index varies directly with the loop index.)

Local Variables

A local variable has the following property:

- The variable is initialized in each loop iteration before its value is used.

The following example loop contains both shared and local variables. (Assume that the outermost loop is the one to be executed in parallel.)

```
         DO 10 i = 1,n
         DO 10 k = 1,n
         DO 10 j = 1,n
            R(i,j) = R(i,j) + S(i,k) * T(k,j)
   10    CONTINUE
```

In this loop, the variables R, S, T, and n are all shared. S, T, and n are all read-only, and R is an array whose index varies directly with the loop index. The variables k and j are not read-only. However, they do meet the requirement for local variables: they are initialized by each iteration before they are used in any operation.

Reduction Variables

A reduction variable is an array or scalar variable that has the following properties:

- It is used in only one associative, commutative operation within the loop. (These operations include addition/subtraction, multiplication/division, logical AND, logical OR, and exclusive OR.)

NOTE

For reduction variables, subtraction and division are treated as addition and multiplication of inverses.

- The operation is of the form:

    var = var op expr

where *var* is the reduction variable, *op* is an associative, commutative operation, and *expr* is an expression that does not include the variable *var*. The variable may occur in more than one such statement, as long as the operation is the same.

The following example loop contains a reduction variable:

```
      DO 66666 k = 1,i-1
         Q = Q + B(i,k) * W(i-k)
66666    CONTINUE
```

In this loop, the variables B, W, and i are shared, because they are read-only within the loop. The variable Q is a reduction variable. It is used in a single associative, commutative operation (addition) and the operation has the correct form.

Shared Ordered Variables

A shared ordered variable is an array or scalar variable that has the following properties:

- It does not qualify as a shared, local, or reduction variable.

- If the loop iterations were executed one at a time in random order, the operations involving the variable would not produce correct results.

The following example loop contains two shared ordered variables.

```
do 10 i = 1, n
   x(i) = xa(i) + xb(i)
   dx = x(i) - x(i-1)
   y(i) = ya(i) + yb(i)
   dy = y(i) - y(i-1)
   rho(i) = sqrt(dx * dx + dy * dy)
10 continue
```

In this loop, the variables xa, xb, ya, and yb are shared, because they are all read-only. The variables dx and dy are local because they are initialized in each loop iteration before their values are used. The variables x and y are shared ordered. If the loop iterations were executed in random order, the operations involving x and y would produce different values than when the loop is executed in sequential order.

Shared Locked Variables

Shared locked variables include all the variables that do not fit into any of the other four categories. A shared locked variable is an array or scalar variable that has the following properties:

- It can be read and written by more than one loop iteration.

- If the loop iterations were executed one at a time in random order, the operations involving the variable would produce correct results.

The first of these characteristics makes the difference between a simple shared variable and a shared locked variable. Because a shared locked variable can be read and written by more than one loop iteration and because we intend to execute loop iterations simultaneously, we have to ensure that only one loop iteration is using the variable at a time. The mechanism to do this is a lock, hence the name *shared locked variable*.

The following example computes the distance between one city and a number of other cities, then compares each distance with the minimum distance and selects the array index of the nearest city. This loop contains one shared ordered variable:

```
        x = 1
        y = 2
        least = 9999999.0
        DO 10 i = 1,n
            xsqdis = (BVRTN(x)-A(i,x))**2
            ysqdis = (BVRTN(y)-A(i,y))**2
            dist = SQRT(xsqdis + ysqdis)
            IF (dist.LT.least) THEN
                closest = i
                least = dist
            ENDIF
10      CONTINUE
```

In this loop, the variables `bvrtn` and `A` are shared: they are read-only within the loop. The variables `xsqdis`, `ysqdis`, and `dist` are local, they are written before they are read in each iteration. The variables `closest` and `least` are shared locked. They are read and written by each loop iteration, but the order in which the iterations are executed does not affect the results of the operations involving them. As long as the loop is executed n times, `dist` will be compared with each value of `least`. As long as nothing changes the value of `closest` or `least` between the IF statement and either assignment statement, the loop will return the correct answers.

Variable Analysis Worksheet

As you analyze the variables in your loop, you may find it helpful to use the worksheet shown in Figure 4-1.

VARIABLE NAME	SHARED	LOCAL	REDUCTION	SHARED ORDERED	SHARED LOCKED
	Is the variable read-only within the loop OR is it an array where each element is read and written by only one loop iteration?	*Could the variable be renamed in each iteration without affecting the program result?*	*Is the variable used in only one associative, commutative operation within the loop AND is it always read, then written?*	*If the loop iterations were exectued in random order, would the operations involving this variable produce different results?*	*Have you answered "no" to all the other questions?*

1003−45453A

Fig. 4-1. Variable analysis worksheet.

To use this worksheet, simply list all the variables in your loop in the first column. For each variable, mark in the answers to the listed questions until you answer "yes" to a question. When you mark a "yes" in any column, you'll find the variable type in the label at the top of the column. Section 4.2.2 shows some completed worksheets.

4.2.2 Preparing the Loop

Once you have analyzed the variables in your loop, you are ready to use
the FORTRAN parallel programming directives to prepare the loop for
parallel execution. Table 4-1 lists the five parallel programming directives.

Table 4-1
Parallel Programming Directives

Directives	Descriptions
C$DOACROSS	Identify DO loop for parallel execution.
C$ORDER	Start loop section which contains a shared ordered variable.
C$ENDORDER	End loop section which contains a shared ordered variable.
C$	Add FORTRAN statement for conditional compilation.
C$&	Continue parallel programming directive.

If your loop has any shared locked variables, you will also use the
DYNIX Parallel Programming Library routines m_lock and m_unlock
to mark the loop sections containing the shared ordered variables.

Marking the Parallel Loop

The first step in preparing the loop for parallel execution is to add a
C$DOACROSS directive on the line immediately preceding the DO state-
ment. The C$DOACROSS directive looks like this:

    C$DOACROSS option[,option...]

The directive has six options: SHARE, LOCAL, REDUCTION, ORDER,
UNROLL, and CHUNK. The SHARE, LOCAL, and REDUCTION options are
used to declare the names and types of all the variables in the loop. The
ORDER option is used to declare names for loop sections containing shared
ordered variables. The UNROLL option is used to minimize loop control
overhead, and the CHUNK option is used to minimize scheduling overhead. (For more information on the UNROLL and CHUNK options, refer
to the *Sequent FORTRAN Compiler User's Manual*.)

To mark a loop with the C$DOACROSS directive, follow this procedure:

1. Insert a C$DOACROSS directive on the line before the DO statement.

2. Add the SHARE option to the C$DOACROSS statement and list in parentheses all the shared, shared ordered, and shared locked variables from your worksheet.

3. If your loop includes any local variables, add the LOCAL option and list in parentheses all the local variables from the worksheet.

4. If your loop includes any reduction variables, add the REDUCTION option and list in parentheses all the reduction variables from the worksheet.

5. If the loop contains any shared ordered variables, add the ORDER option, choose names for the loop sections containing the variables, and list the names in parentheses. You can use any valid FORTRAN name for an ordered section.

If the C$DOACROSS directive is too long, you can use the C$& directive to continue it onto a new line.

Let's look at an example loop from Section 4.2.1 and see how to mark it with a C$DOACROSS directive. The following example, a matrix product, has four shared variables and two local variables:

```
          DO 10 i = 1,n
          DO 10 k = 1,n
          DO 10 j = 1,n
             R(i,j) = R(i,j) + S(i,k) * T(k,j)
      10    CONTINUE
```

Figure 4-2 shows the completed variable analysis worksheet for this loop. Notice that the programmer has not included the loop index, i, in the analysis. Only j and k, the indices of the inner loops, are included.

VARIABLE NAME	SHARED	LOCAL	REDUCTION	SHARED ORDERED	SHARED LOCKED
	Is the variable read-only within the loop OR is it an array where each element is read and written by only one loop iteration?	*Could the variable be renamed in each iteration without affecting the program result?*	*Is the variable used in only one associative, commutative operation within the loop AND is it always read, then written?*	*If the loop iterations were exectued in random order, would the operations involving this variable produce different results?*	*Have you answered "no" to all the other questions?*
k	no	yes			
j	no	yes			
n	yes				
R	yes				
S	yes				
T	yes				

1003-45454A

Fig. 4-2. Variable analysis worksheet for independent loop.

When the C$DOACROSS statement is added, using the information from the worksheet, the loop looks like this:

```
C$DOACROSS SHARE(R, S, T, n), LOCAL(k, j)
          DO 10 i = 1,n
          DO 10 k = 1,n
          DO 10 j = 1,n
             R(i,j) = R(i,j) + S(i,k) * T(k,j)
     10   CONTINUE
```

NOTE

Notice that the C$DOACROSS directive starts in column 1, just like a FORTRAN comment line. Thus, if you run the FORTRAN compiler without the parallel (-mp) option, the compiler treats these directives as comment statements.

Marking Ordered Sections

The C$ORDER and C$ENDORDER directives mark the beginning and end of a loop section containing a shared ordered variable. The C$ORDER directive appears on the line immediately preceding the first reference to the variable, and the C$ENDORDER directive appears on the line immediately following the last reference to the variable. (Actually, there are more exact rules for placing these directives for highly optimized execution, but such placement requires more complex evaluation of the order dependency. Refer to Appendix B for a discussion of this evaluation.)

These directives look like this:

```
C$ORDER section_name
C$ENDORDER section_name
```

The *section_name* parameter can be any valid FORTRAN name. The section name in the C$ENDORDER directive must match the name in the corresponding C$ORDER directive, and both must match a name declared with the C$DOACROSS ORDER option. The section name cannot be used for any other purpose within the program.

NOTE

You must ensure that each C$ORDER/C$ENDORDER pair is executed exactly once by each loop iteration. Each loop iteration waits at a C$ORDER directive for the previous iteration to execute the corresponding C$ENDORDER directive before executing the ordered section. If an iteration fails to execute an ordered section (e.g., because of a conditional branch), the subsequent iterations can never execute that ordered section, and the program hangs. If a parallel loop contains a conditional branch, you can place a pair of identical C$ORDER/C$ENDORDER directives within each branch. The duplicate pair can enclose an empty section.

Now let's complete the example ordered loop from Section 4.2.1. This example has four shared variables, two local variables, and two shared ordered variables:

```
do 10 i = 1, n
   x(i) = xa(i) + xb(i)
   dx = x(i) - x(i-1)
   y(i) = ya(i) + yb(i)
   dy = y(i) - y(i-1)
   rho(i) = sqrt(dx * dx + dy * dy)
10   continue
```

Figure 4-3 shows the completed variable analysis worksheet for this loop.

VARIABLE NAME	SHARED	LOCAL	REDUCTION	SHARED ORDERED	SHARED LOCKED
	Is the variable read-only within the loop OR is it an array where each element is read and written by only one loop iteration?	*Could the variable be renamed in each iteration without affecting the program result?*	*Is the variable used in only one associative, commutative operation within the loop AND is it always read, then written?*	*If the loop iterations were executed in random order, would the operations involving this variable produce different results?*	*Have you answered "no" to all the other questions?*
xa	yes				
xb	yes				
ya	yes				
yb	yes				
x	no	no	no	yes	
y	no	no	no	yes	
dx	no	yes			
dy	no	yes			
rho	yes				

1003-45455A

Fig. 4-3. Variable analysis worksheet for ordered loop.

When the C$DOACROSS statement is added, using the information from the worksheet, the loop looks like this:

```
c$doacross order(gx,gy),share(x,xa,xb, y,ya,yb, rho),
c$& local(dx, dy)
      do 10 i = 1, n
        x(i) = xa(i) + xb(i)
        dx = x(i) - x(i-1)
        y(i) = ya(i) + yb(i)
        dy = y(i) - y(i-1)
        rho(i) = sqrt(dx * dx + dy * dy)
10    continue
```

In this example, the programmer has chosen the names gx and gy for the code sections containing the variables x and y. To complete the preparation of this loop, the programmer must include C$ORDER and C$ENDORDER directives to mark the ordered sections. With the C$ORDER and C$ENDORDER directives added, the loop looks like this:

```
c$doacross order(gx,gy),share(x,xa,xb, y,ya,yb, rho),
c$& local(dx, dy)
      do 10 i = 1, n
c$order gx
        x(i) = xa(i) + xb(i)
        dx = x(i) - x(i-1)
c$endorder gx
c$order gy
        y(i) = ya(i) + yb(i)
        dy = y(i) - y(i-1)
c$endorder gy
        rho(i) = sqrt(dx * dx + dy * dy + dz * dz)
10    continue
```

Marking Locked Sections

The DYNIX Parallel Programming Library routines m_lock and m_unlock mark the beginning and end of a loop section containing a shared locked variable. The m_lock directive should appear on the line immediately preceding the first reference to the variable, and the m_unlock directive should appear on the line immediately following the last reference to the variable.

Calls to these routines look like this:

```
CALL m_lock
CALL m_unlock
```

You may want the m_lock and m_unlock calls compiled only when the parallel option is specified. To do this, begin the call statements with the c$ directive. (This directive allows you to insert any valid FORTRAN statement into a program and have it compiled only when the preprocessor is invoked.)

Now let's complete the example ordered loop from Section 4.2.1. This example has two shared locked variables. (Assume that the variable closest has been declared as an integer.)

```
          x = 1
          y = 2
      least = 9999999.1
      DO 10 i = 1,n
          xsqdis = (BVRTN(x)-A(i,x))**2
          ysqdis = (BVRTN(y)-A(i,y))**2
            dist = SQRT(xsqdis + ysqdis)
          IF (dist.LT.least) THEN
          closest = i
            least = dist
          ENDIF
  10      CONTINUE
```

Figure 4-4 shows the completed variable analysis worksheet for this loop.

VARIABLE NAME	SHARED *Is the variable read-only within the loop OR is it an array where each element is read and written by only one loop iteration?*	LOCAL *Could the variable be renamed in each iteration without affecting the program result?*	REDUCTION *Is the variable used in only one associative, commutative operation within the loop AND is it always read, then written?*	SHARED ORDERED *If the loop iterations were exectued in random order, would the operations involving this variable produce different results?*	SHARED LOCKED *Have you answered "no" to all the other questions?*
BVRTN	yes				
A	yes				
xsqdis	no	yes			
ysqdis	no	yes			
dist	no	yes			
closest	no	no	no	no	yes
least	no	no	no	no	yes
x	yes				
y	yes				

1003-45456A

Fig. 4-4. Variable analysis worksheet for shared locked loop.

When the C$DOACROSS statement is added, using the information from the worksheet, the loop looks like this:

```
                  x = 1
                  y = 2
              least = 9999999.1
C$DOACROSS SHARE(bvrtn, A,closest,least,x,y),
C$&                 LOCAL(xsqdis,ysqdis,dist)
           DO 10 i = 1,n
              xsqdis = (BVRTN(x)-A(i,x))**2
              ysqdis = (BVRTN(y)-A(i,y))**2
                dist = SQRT(xsqdis + ysqdis)
              IF (dist.LT.least) THEN
              closest = i
                least = dist
              ENDIF
    10     CONTINUE
```

NOTE

*Notice the use of the C$& directive to continue the
C$DOACROSS directive to a new line.*

To complete the preparation of this loop, the programmer must include
calls to the Parallel Programming Library routines m_lock and
m_unlock in order to protect the section containing closest and
least. With the m_lock and m_unlock directives added, the loop
looks like this:

```
                  x = 1
                  y = 2
              least = 9999999.1
C$DOACROSS SHARE(bvrtn, A,closest,least,x,y),
C$&                 LOCAL(xsqdis,ysqdis,dist)
           DO 10 i = 1,n
              xsqdis = (BVRTN(x)-A(i,x))**2
              ysqdis = (BVRTN(y)-A(i,y))**2
                dist = SQRT(xsqdis + ysqdis)
C$         CALL m_lock
              IF (dist.LT.least) THEN
              closest = i
                least = dist
              ENDIF
C$         CALL m_unlock
    10     CONTINUE
```

The m_lock and m_unlock routines ensure that only one loop iteration
can execute the locked section at a time.

4.3. Compiling, Executing, and Debugging

To complete development of your data-partitioned FORTRAN program, follow this procedure:

1.   Invoke the FORTRAN compiler with the parallel option. It restructures the source code for data partitioning, and the compiler then produces parallel object code.

2.   Execute the program and check the results.

3.   If necessary, use the DYNIX parallel symbolic debugger, Pdbx, to debug the program.

4.3.1 Compiling the Program

To preprocess, compile, and link a program, enter the following command:

> **fortran -mp** *program.name*

When this command is executed, the parallel preprocessor converts each designated DO loop to run in parallel and places the restructured source code in a file named with the suffix "*.fpp*". The compiler then compiles this new source file in place of the original source and links the object code to produce an executable file named *a.out*. The compiler normally deletes the *.fpp* file after compilation; however, you can use the **-u, -g,** or **-gv** compiler option to save the file for debugging purposes.

If you link the program separately from the compile step, you will use the DYNIX linker, **ld**, and the **-lpps** linker option.

For more information on the FORTRAN compiler and its options, refer to the *Sequent FORTRAN Compiler User's Manual*. For more information on the DYNIX linker, refer to the *ld(1)* man page in the *DYNIX Programmer's Manual, Vol. 1*.

4.3.2 Executing the Program

To execute the program, simply enter the name of the executable file, *a.out*, as a DYNIX command.

4.3.3 Debugging the Program

If your program produces incorrect results, you can use the DYNIX Pdbx debugger to isolate any problems. Pdbx is a high-level language symbolic debugger based on dbx, a debugger widely used in UNIX systems.

When debugging your program, refer to the *.fpp* file created by the parallel preprocessor. This file contains FORTRAN source code with your parallel loops restructured as subroutines. The subroutine names are derived from the label of the loop termination statement. If you set debugger breakpoints within your parallel loops, the debugger uses the contents of the *.fpp* file as the source code.

For more information on Pdbx, refer to the *Sequent Pdbx User's Manual*.

4.4. Additional Sources of Information

The following sources provide information that may be helpful to you:

- The *Sequent FORTRAN Compiler User's Manual* describes in detail the Sequent FORTRAN language, the compiler and its options, and the parallel programming directives.

- The *DYNIX Programmer's Manual* provides more detailed descriptions of the DYNIX Parallel Programming Library routines and the DYNIX linker, **ld**.

- The *Sequent Pdbx User's Manual* provides instructions for using the Pdbx debugger and reference information on the debugger command set.

- Chapter 2 presents parallel programming terms and concepts.

- Chapter 5 explains how to do data partitioning on other kinds of loops in C, Pascal, and FORTRAN programs.

- Appendices A and B discuss factors that may affect the execution speed of your program.

- Appendix D contains the Parallel Programming Library man pages.

- Appendix E lists other literature on parallel programming.

Chapter 5

Data Partitioning with DYNIX

Tables

Table No.   Page

Illustrations

Fig. No.   Page

Chapter 5

Data Partitioning with DYNIX

5.1. Introduction

This chapter explains how to structure C, FORTRAN, and Pascal programs for data partitioning, and how to use the DYNIX Parallel Programming Library to execute loops in parallel. (Sequent FORTRAN includes special directives for data partitioning of DO loops. If you wish to data partition a FORTRAN DO loop, refer to Chapter 4.)

This chapter is organized as follows:

- Section 5.2 introduces the data partitioning method called *microtasking*.

- Section 5.3 introduces the Parallel Programming Library routines.

- Section 5.4 explains how to analyze data flow within a loop.

- Section 5.5 explains how to structure a microtasking program.

- Section 5.6 briefly explains how to compile, load, execute, and debug your program.

- Section 5.7 lists additional sources of information.

NOTES

Most examples in this chapter are in C or Pascal. The discussion and instructions apply to FORTRAN, C, and Pascal programs except where noted.

The Parallel Programming Library is compatible with Sequent Pascal,pascal(1), not with Berkeley Pascal, pc(1).

5.2. The Microtasking Method

The data-partitioning method described in this chapter is sometimes called *microtasking*. Microtasking programs create multiple independent processes to execute loop iterations in parallel. The microtasking method has the following characteristics:

- The parallel processes share some data and create their own private copies of other data.

- The division of the computing load adjusts automatically to the number of available processes.

- The program controls data flow and synchronization by using tools specially designed for data partitioning.

You determine which data is shared between parallel processes and how the program adjusts to the number of available CPUs. (Sections 5.4 and 5.5 explain how to do this.) The Parallel Programming Library contains the tools to create and control parallel processes in your microtasking program.

A microtasking program works like this:

- Each loop to be executed in parallel is contained in a subprogram.

- For each loop, the program calls a special function which forks a set of child processes and assigns an identical copy of the subprogram to each process for parallel execution. The special function creates a copy of any private data for each process.

- Each copy of the subprogram executes some of the loop iterations. You can set up the subprogram to use either static scheduling or dynamic scheduling.

- If the loop being executed in parallel is not completely independent, the subprogram may contain calls to functions that synchronize the parallel processes at critical points by using locks, barriers, and other semaphores.

- When all the loop iterations have been executed, control returns from the subprogram. At this point, the program either terminates the parallel processes, suspends their execution until they are needed to execute another subprogram, or leaves them to spin in a *busy wait* state until they are needed again.

5.3. The Parallel Programming Library

The DYNIX Parallel Programming Library includes three sets of routines: a microtasking library, a set of routines for general use with data partitioning programs, and a set of routines for memory allocation in data partitioning programs. Appendix E contains the DYNIX man pages for the Parallel Programming Library routines.

5.3.1 The Microtasking Library

The microtasking library routines allow you to fork a set of child processes, assign the processes to execute loop iterations in parallel, and synchronize the processes as necessary to provide proper data flow between loop iterations. Table 5-1 lists the microtasking routines in the Parallel Programming Library.

Table 5-1
Parallel Programming Library Microtasking Routines

Routines	Descriptions
m_fork	Execute a subprogram in parallel.
m_get_myid	Return process identification number.
m_get_numprocs	Return number of child processes.
m_kill_procs	Terminate child processes.
m_lock	Lock a lock.
m_multi	End single-process code section.
m_next	Increment global counter.
m_park_procs	Suspend child process execution.
m_rele_procs	Resume child process execution.
m_set_procs	Set number of child processes.
m_single	Begin single-process code section.
m_sync	Check in at barrier.
m_unlock	Unlock a lock.

NOTE

The microtasking library is designed around the m_fork *routine. The other microtasking routines should be used only in combination with the* m_fork *routine. Otherwise, they can cause unexpected side effects.*

5.3.2 Data Partitioning Library

The general-purpose data-partitioning routines include a routine to determine the number of available CPUs and several process synchronization routines that are more flexible than those available in the microtasking library. Table 5-2 lists the general-purpose data-partitioning routines in the Parallel Programming Library.

Table 5-2
Parallel Programming Library Data-Partitioning Routines

Routines	Descriptions
cpus_online	Return number of CPUs on-line.
s_init_barrier	Initialize a barrier.
S_INIT_BARRIER	C macro.
s_init_lock	Initialize a lock.
S_INIT_LOCK	C macro.
s_lock or s_clock	Lock a lock.
S_LOCK or s_CLOCK	C macros.
s_unlock	Unlock a lock.
S_UNLOCK	C macro.
s_wait_barrier	Wait at a barrier.
S_WAIT_BARRIER	C macro.

5.3.3 Memory Allocation Routines

The memory allocation routines allow a data-partitioning program to allocate and de-allocate shared memory and to change the amount of shared and private memory assigned to a process. Table 5-3 lists the memory allocation routines in the Parallel Programming Library.

Table 5-3
Parallel Programming Library Memory-Allocation Routines

Routines	Descriptions
brk or sbrk	Change private data segment size.
shbrk or shsbrk	Change shared data segment size.
shfree	De-allocate shared data memory.
shmalloc	Allocate shared data memory.

Section 5.5 explains how to use the Parallel Programming Library routines in a program and presents some sample programs. For a detailed reference to the Parallel Programming Library, refer to Section 3P in Volume 1 of the *DYNIX Programmer's Manual*.

5.4. Analyzing Variable Usage

Before you can convert a loop into a subprogram for data partitioning, you must analyze all the variables in the loop and determine two things:

- Which data can be shared between parallel processes and which must be local to each parallel process.

- Which variables cause dependences or *critical regions*, code sections which can yield incorrect results when executed in parallel.

(If you have already read Chapter 4, you are familiar with the information presented in this section. You may wish to turn directly to Section 5.5.)

5.4.1 Shared Variables and Private Variables

A variable must be private if it is initialized in each loop iteration before it is used. All other variables are shared. Private variables are usually scalar (single-element) variables, although other data structures may be private.

The following sample matrix multiply loop contains both shared and private variables. (Assume that the outermost loop is the one to be executed in parallel.)

```
for (i=0; i<n; i++)
    for (k=0; k<n; k++)
        for (j=0; j<n; j++)
            r[i][j] = r[i][j] + s[i][k] * t[k][j];
```

In this loop, the variables i, k, and j are local: they are initialized at the beginning of each loop iteration before they are used. (Remember that we are referring to the outermost loop.)

Once you have identified the private variables, you can declare the shared and private variables in your program. In C, you do this by using the keywords **shared** and **private** in declaration statements. In FORTRAN, you do this by placing all the shared variables in one or more COMMON blocks and then using the **-F** compiler option to declare those COMMON blocks to be shared. In Pascal, you use the **-mp** compiler option to make all global variables shared and all local variables private.

In C, you need to define only static or external variables to be shared or private. Automatic variables are handled correctly for you, and register variables cannot be shared. To declare a variable as shared or private, simply add the keyword shared or private to the variable's declaration statement. For more information on the shared and private keywords, refer to the *Sequent C Compiler User's Manual*.

In FORTRAN programs, all variables are treated as private unless they are explicitly declared to be shared. (This assumes the program is not compiled with the **-mp** option.) Therefore you must place all shared variables in shared COMMON blocks. Section 5.6.1 explains how to use the **-F** option to declare which COMMON blocks are shared.

Section 5.6.1 also explains how to use the **-mp** Pascal compiler option.

5.4.2 Identifying Dependent Variables

Dependent variables are shared variables that can be read and written by more than one loop iteration. These variables can sometimes pass incorrect information between loop iterations if the iterations are executed out of order or if two loop iterations try to write the variable simultaneously. This section explains how to identify these variables and Section 5.5 presents some special tools and techniques for handling dependent variables to ensure correct results.

You can use the following simple tests to determine whether a shared variable is dependent:

- Is it a *read-only* variable; in other words, is it read but never written within the loop?

- Is it an array in which each element is referenced by only one loop iteration? (This occurs when the array index varies directly with the loop index.)

If the answer to either of these questions is "yes," then the variable is independent and you simply declare it as shared. If the answer is "no," then the variable is dependent and you need to determine the type of its dependence.

Dependent variables fall into the following three categories:

- Reduction variables

- Ordered variables

- Locked variables

The remainder of this section explains how to identify these types of dependent variables. Section 5.5.2 describes techniques for handling each type of dependence in your program.

Reduction Variables

A reduction variable is an array or scalar variable that has the following properties:

- It is used in only one associative, commutative operation within the loop. These operations include addition, multiplication, logical AND, logical OR, and exclusive OR.

- In C or FORTRAN programs, the operation is of the form:

    var = var op expr

  In C programs it may also be of the form:

    var op= expr

  In Pascal programs, the operation is of the form:

    var := var op expr

  where *var* is the reduction variable, *op* is an associative, commutative operation, and *expr* is an expression that does not include the variable *var*. The variable may occur in more that one such statement, as long as the operation is consistent.

The following example loop contains a reduction variable:

```
for (k=0; k<i-1; k++)
    q = q + b[i][k] * w[i-k];
```

In this loop, the variables b, w, and i are independent, because they are read-only within the loop. The variable q is a reduction variable. It is used in a single associative, commutative operation (addition) and the operation has the correct form. (The loop index, k, is local.)

Locked Variables

A locked variable is an array or scalar variable that has the following properties:

- The variable can be read and written by more than one loop iteration.

- If the loop iterations were executed one at a time in random order, the operations involving the variable would produce correct results.

Because a locked variable can be read and written by more than one loop iteration and because we intend to execute loop iterations simultaneously, we have to ensure that only one loop iteration is using the variable at a time. The mechanism to do this is called a lock, hence the name locked variable.

The following example computes the distance between one city and a number of other cities, then compares each distance with the minimum distance, and selects the array index of the nearest city. This loop contains one locked variable.

```
x = 0
y = 1
least = 999999;
for (i=1; i<n; i++) {
    xsqdis = sq(bvrtn[x]-a[i][x]);
    ysqdis = sq(bvrtn[y]-a[i][y]);
    dist   = sqrt(xsqdis + ysqdis);
    if (dist < least) {
        closest = i;
        least   = dist;
    }
}
```

In this loop, the variables bvrtn and a are independent shared variables: they are read-only within the loop. The variables xsqdis, ysqdis, and dist are local: they are written in each iteration before they are read. The variables closest and least must be locked. They are read and written by each loop iteration, but the order in which the iterations are executed does not affect the results of the operations involving them. As long as the loop is executed n times, each value of dist will be compared with least. As long as nothing changes the value of closest or least between the if statement and either assignment statement, the loop will return the correct answers.

Ordered Variables

An ordered variable is an array or scalar variable that has the following property:

- The loop consistently yields correct results only if the operations involving the variable are executed one iteration at a time, in serial order.

The following example loop contains two ordered variables.

```
for (i=0; i < n; i++ ) {
    x(i) = xa(i) + xb(i);
    dx = x(i) - x(i-1);
    y(i) = ya(i) + yb(i);
    dy = y(i) - y(i-1);
    rho(i) = sqrt(dx * dx + dy * dy);
}
```

In this loop, the variables xa, xb, ya, and yb are shared, because they are all read-only. The variables dx and dy are local because they are initialized in each loop iteration before their values are used. The variables x and y are ordered. If the loop iterations were executed in random order, the operations involving x and y would produce different values than when the loop is executed in sequential order.

5.4.3 Variable Analysis Worksheet

As you analyze the variables in your loop, you may find it helpful to use the worksheet shown in in Figure 5-1.

	SHARED	LOCAL	REDUCTION	SHARED ORDERED	SHARED LOCKED
VARIABLE NAME	*Is the variable read-only within the loop OR is it an array where each element is read and written by only one loop iteration?*	*Could the variable be renamed in each iteration without affecting the program result?*	*Is the variable used in only one associative, commutative operation within the loop AND is it always read, then written?*	*If the loop iterations were exectued in random order, would the operations involving this variable produce different results?*	*Have you answered "no" to all the other questions?*

1003-45453A

Fig. 5-1. Variable analysis worksheet.

To use this worksheet, simply list all the variables in your loop in the first column. For each variable, mark your answers to the listed questions until you either answer "yes" to one question or run out of questions. When you mark a "yes" in any column, you'll find the variable type in the label at the top of the column.

5.5. The Microtasking Program

This section explains how to structure a microtasking program. In such a program, each loop to be executed in parallel is contained in a subprogram which we will call the *looping subprogram*. Section 5.5.1 describes the calling program, Section 5.5.2 describes the looping subprogram, Section 5.5.3 discusses shared memory allocation, and Section 5.5.4 presents some complete program examples.

5.5.1 The Calling Program

The calling program handles the following tasks:

- Including any header files required by the Parallel Programming Library routines (C programs only).

- Determining how many parallel processes are created to execute the loop. This determination is based on the number of CPUs in the system. The program can either call the Parallel Programming library routine `m_set_procs` or it can use the default number computed by the Parallel Programming Library.

- Calling the Parallel Programming Library routine `m_fork` to execute each looping subprogram in parallel.

- Suspending or terminating parallel processes between calls to looping subprograms, and terminating all parallel processes after the last looping subprogram has been executed.

Parallel Programming Library Header File

DYNIX includes two C header files which contain declaration statements for the Parallel Proramming Library routines. One file contains declarations for the microtasking routines and the other contains declarations for the other routines. Both of these header files reside in the directory */usr/include/parallel*. The header files are named *microtask.h* and *parallel.h*. Refer to Section 3P in the *DYNIX Programmer's Manual* for information on which file to include for a specific routine.

Determining How Many Parallel Processes to Use

To determine how many parallel processes your program will use to execute the loop subprogram, you can either call the Parallel Programming Library routine `m_set_procs` or you can use a default number computed by the Parallel Prorgamming Library. The `m_set_procs` function sets the number of processes that will exist after subsequent calls to the routine `m_fork`. (This number includes the parent process.) If your program uses `m_set_procs`, you may want to also use the routine `cpus_online` to find out how many CPUs are currently on line.

By default, the number of processes created by `m_fork` is equal to the number of CPUs on-line divided by two. By using the `m_set_procs` function, you can set this number as low as one or as high as the number of CPUs on-line minus 1.

In C, the calls to the **cpus_online** and *m_set_procs* functions look like this:

```
var = cpus_online();

val = m_set_procs(nprocs);
```

In Pascal, the calls to these functions look like this:

```
var := cpus_online();

val := m_set_procs(nprocs);
```

In FORTRAN, the calls to these functions look like this:

```
var = cpus_online()

val = m_set_procs(nprocs)
```

The variables *var*, *val*, and *nprocs* must all be of type `int` in C programs, type `longint` in Pascal programs, and type `INTEGER*4` in FORTRAN programs.

Calling the Looping Subprogram: The m_fork Routine

The Parallel Programming Library function `m_fork` executes the looping subprogram in parallel. `M_fork` creates processes or reuses a set of existing processes and assigns them to execute copies of the specified loop subprogram. It can also pass an argument list to each copy.

In C, the `m_fork` function call looks like this:

```
m_fork(func[,arg,...]);
```

In Pascal, the `m_fork` function call looks like this:

```
m_pfork(func[,arg,...]);
```

In FORTRAN, the `m_fork` function call looks like this:

```
external func
call m_fork(func[,arg,...])
```

The *func* argument is the name of the looping subprogram and the arguments *arg* are its parameters. These parameters can be of any type. In a C program, you must declare the `m_fork` function to be of type `void`.

When the `m_fork` function is called, it determines whether there are existing child processes, processes created by a previous `m_fork` call. If there are existing child processes, it reuses them to execute the loop subprogram. If not, it creates a new set of child processes to execute the subprogram.

The `m_fork` routine creates enough child processes to bring the total number of processes (including the parent process) to either the default (number of CPUs on-line/2) or the number you set with a previous call to the `m_set_procs` function. As `m_fork` creates child processes, it assigns each process a private integer variable called *m_myid*, which uniquely indentifies that child process within the set of processes belonging to that program. The main program (the parent process) has the *m_myid* value 0, the first child process created has the *m_myid* value 1, and so on. You can find the identification number of any process by calling the Parallel Programming Library function `m_get_myid`.

Once child processes are available, `m_fork` passes them copies of their parameters and starts them executing the looping subprogram *func*. When all the child processes are started, the parent process gives itself a copy of the loop subprogram and parameters, and all the processes execute the loop subprogram until they all return from it. At this point, the child processes spin, waiting for more work. The parent process can either kill the child processes, suspend them, or let them spin until they are reused by another `m_fork` call.

Re-using and Terminating Parallel Processes

As explained in Section 5.2, a program typically forks as many child processes as it needs at the beginning and does not terminate them until all parallel computation is complete. The Parallel Programming Library includes three routines to manage child processes after `m_fork` calls: `m_park_procs`, `m_rele_procs`, and `m_kill_procs`. By default, after the program returns from an `m_fork` call, the child processes spin, using CPU time. If your program requires a lot of computation before the next `m_fork` call, it can suspend the child processes and relinquish their CPUs for use by other processes by calling the `m_park_procs` routine.

The program then resumes child process execution by calling the
m_rele_procs routine. After the last m_fork call, the program should
call the routine m_kill_procs to terminate the child processes.

5.5.2 The Looping Subprogram

This section explains how to construct a looping subprogram. In addition
to executing a loop in parallel, the looping subprogram handles the following tasks:

- *Scheduling*, determining which process will execute which loop
  iterations .

- Protecting code sections that contain dependent variables so
  that they yield correct results.

- Synchronizing processes as necessary.

- Handling I/O, if required.

Static and Dynamic Scheduling

In data-partitioning programs, you can use either static or dynamic
scheduling. Static scheduling requires no communication between
processes. Dynamic scheduling requires more communication, but can
even out an unbalanced computing load.

Static Scheduling. If you know that the computing time is approximately the same for each iteration of your loop, you can use static
scheduling. The static scheduling algorithm simply divides the loop
iterations evenly among the processes.

The static scheduling algorithm for a process involves the following
steps:

1. Call the Parallel Programming Library routine
   m_get_numprocs to determine how many processes were
   created by the m_fork call. (We'll call this number M.)

2. Call the Parallel Programming library routine m_get_myid to
   find out my process ID number. (We'll call this number N.)

3. Start by executing the Nth loop iteration.

4. Execute every *Mth* iteration until I reach the end of the loop.

Refer to Section 5.5.4 for an example program that uses static scheduling.

Dynamic Scheduling. If you know that the computing time varies for each iteration of your loop, you can use dynamic scheduling. With dynamic scheduling, the loop iterations are treated as a task queue, and each process removes one or more iterations from the queue, executes those iterations, and returns for more work. This method is sometimes called "hungry puppies" because the processes "nibble" away at the work until it is all done.

Dynamic scheduling creates more communication overhead than static scheduling because all the processes must access a single shared task queue, but the computing load can be very evenly distributed because no process is idle while there is still work to be done. For data partitioning, the task queue can be implemented by using the `m_next` routine.

A typical dynamic scheduling algorithm includes the following steps:

1. Lock a lock.

2. Check shared loop index and verify that there is still work to be done.

3. Increment or decrement the shared loop index by N. (The `m_next` routine is useful for this if your shared loop index can start at zero and increment.)

4. Unlock the lock.

5. Execute N iterations.

6. Repeat steps 1 through 5 until all the work is finished.

If you use the `m_next` routine, you do not need to explicitly lock and unlock a lock. These steps are built into `m_next`. Refer to Section 5.5.4 for an example program that uses `m_next` in dynamic scheduling.

Handling Dependent Variables

This section describes techniques for handling order, reduction, and lock-type data dependencies.

Handling Locked Sections. If your loop contains locked variables, you need to use the Parallel Programming Library routines `m_lock` and `m_unlock` to ensure that the code section containing those variables is executed by only one loop iteration at a time. The `m_lock` call should appear on the line immediately preceding the first reference to a locked variable, and the `m_unlock` call should appear on the line immediately following the last reference to a locked variable.

Refer to Section 5.5.4 for an example program that uses these routines to protect the shared loop index in a dynamically scheduled loop subprogram.

The `m_lock` and `m_unlock` routines support only one lock per looping subprogram. If your program requires more than one lock at a time, you can use the `s_init_lock`, `s_lock` or `s_clock`, and `s_unlock` routines. Refer to the *s_lock*(5P) man page in the *DYNIX Programmer's Manual* for more information on these routines.

Handling Reduction Variables. Reduction variables are similar to locked variables, except that you need to protect them with locks only part of the time. You can create a local reduction variable, initialize it within the parallel loop routine, and substitute the local variable name for the reduction variable name throughout the loop. At the end of the loop subprogram, you can call the `m_lock` function, perform the reduction operation to combine the local reduction variable with the shared reduction variable, and call the `m_unlock` function. This is more efficient than an ordinary locked variable because each process executes the locked section only once.

For example, consider the following example loop from Section 5.4.2:

```
for (k=mystart; k<end; k+=incr)
    q = q + b[i][k];
```

The reduction variable `q` is shared. The loop iterations can be executed in any order, but the loop can produce incorrect results if two processes try to read or write `q` simultaneously. As long as the loop is structured this way, it cannot be executed in parallel. However, if we declare a local variable, `lq`, each process can add its values of `b` to `lq` without affecting any other process. Once each process finishes its calculations, it can lock the shared variable `q`, add its `lq` value, and unlock `q`.

```
lq = 0;
for (k=mystart; k<end; k+=incr)
    lq = lq + b[i][k];
m_lock();
q = q + lq;
m_unlock();
```

Handling Ordered Sections. If your loop contains an ordered variable, you need to ensure that the code sections containing that variable are executed in loop iteration order. To ensure this, repeat the following procedure for each ordered variable in the loop.

1. In the main program, declare a shared integer variable to hold the current loop iteration number. (If the shared ordered variable is named i, you might name the new variable something like iguard.) Initialize the new variable to the starting value of the loop index.

2. In the looping subprogram, on the line before the first reference to the shared ordered variable, insert a conditional statement that loops on itself until the loop index value is equal to the value of the iteration count variable.

3. On the line after the last reference to the shared ordered variable, insert a statement to increment the shared iteration counter variable.

NOTE

At some optimization levels, the C optimizer can remove conditional tests in spin loops. If your codes uses any spin loops on shared variables, always compile with the -i compiler option to ensure that the conditional tests are preserved. For more information on the -i option, refer to cc(1).

If the ordered variable is written and then read more than once within the loop, you can speed up execution by treating each write/read sequence as a different variable. This allows execution to proceed in parallel between ordered sections.

The following example loop from Section 5.4.2 illustrates these modifications. The shared variables x and y are ordered. Assume that we have declared two shared variables named xguard and yguard in the main program and initialized them to zero.

```
for (i=0; i < n; i++ ) {
    while (xguard != i)
        continue;
    x(i) = xa(i) + xb(i);
    dx = x(i) - x(i-1);
    xguard = xguard + 1;
    while (yguard != i)
        continue;
    y(i) = ya(i) + yb(i);
    dy = y(i) - y(i-1);
    yguard = yguard + 1;
    rho(i) = sqrt(dx * dx + dy * dy);
}
```

Synchronizing Processes

A looping subprogram sometimes contains a code section which depends on all the processes having completed execution of the preceding code. For example, a looping subprogram might execute more than one loop on the same set of data, and the algorithm might require that all the processes finish executing the first loop before starting to execute the second loop. In such situations, you can set up barriers to synchronize the processes.

The Parallel Programming Library includes routines to set up two kinds of barriers. The routine m_sync synchronizes all the processes at a single, pre-initialized barrier. To set more than one barrier, or to synchronize a subset of the processes, the looping subprogram can call s_init_barrier to initialize a barrier and then call s_wait_barrier to synchronize processes at the barrier.

Handling I/O

Section 2.9 mentioned the complications of doing I/O from the parallel portion of a program. The Parallel Programming Library allows you to avoid these complications by setting up single-process sections within a looping subprogram. The looping subprogram can call the Parallel Programming Library routine m_single to halt execution of child processes while the parent process performs I/O. It can then call the m_multi routine to start child process execution again. The child processes spin while the parent is doing I/O.

5.5.3 Shared Memory Allocation

The Parallel Programming Library contains a set of routines for dynamic allocation and management of shared memory. For C programs, the shmalloc and shfree routines allocate and release shared memory for data structures whose size is determined at run time. The shmalloc routine returns a shared pointer to the newly allocated shared memory. (In Pascal, dynamic shared memory allocation is handled by the NEW routine, and FORTRAN does not allow dynamic memory allocation.)

The shbrk and shsbrk routines increase the size of a process's shared data segment and verify that the increase does not cause the shared data segment to overlap the process's shared stack. The Parallel Programming Library brk and sbrk routines are used like the standard DYNIX brk and sbrk to increase a process's private data segment size, but they also verify that the increase does not cause the private data segment to overlap the process's shared data segment.

The -Z linker option also allows you to control the size and base address of the shared data segment. For more information on this option, refer to the *ld*(1) man page in the *DYNIX Programmer's Manual*.

5.5.4 Example Programs

Static Scheduling - C Example

```
/* multiply two matrices, store results in third matrix,
   and print results */

#include <stdio.h>
#include <parallel/microtask.h>  /* microtasking header */
#include <parallel/parallel.h>   /* parallel lib header */
#define SIZE 10                   /* size of matrices */

     /* Global shared memory data */

        shared float a[SIZE][SIZE]; /* first array */
        shared float b[SIZE][SIZE]; /* second array */
        shared float c[SIZE][SIZE]; /* result array */

main ()
{
     void init_matrix(), m_fork(), m_kill_procs(),
         matmul(), print_mats();
     int nprocs;  /* number of parallel processes */
```

```
        printf("Enter number of processes:");
        scanf("%d",&nprocs);

        init_matrix(a, b);              /* initialize data */
        m_set_procs(nprocs);            /* set # of processes */
        m_fork(matmul, a, b, c);/* execute parallel loop */
        m_kill_procs();                 /* kill child processes */
        print_mats(a, b, c);            /* print results */
}

/* initialize matrix function */

void
init_matrix(a, b)
float a[][SIZE], b[][SIZE];
{
    int i, j;

    for (i = 0; i < SIZE; i ++) {
        for (j = 0; j < SIZE; j ++) {
            a[i][j] = (float)i + j;
            b[i][j] = (float)i - j;
        }
    }
}

/* matrix multiply function */

void
matmul(a, b, c)
float a[][SIZE], b[][SIZE], c[][SIZE];
{
    int i, j, k, nprocs;

    nprocs = m_get_numprocs();    /* no. of processes */
    for (i = m_get_myid(); i < SIZE; i += nprocs) {
        for (j = 0; j < SIZE; j ++) {
            for (k = 0; k < SIZE; k ++)
                c[i][k] += a[i][j] * b[j][k];
        }
    }
}

/* print results function */

void
print_mats(a, b, c)
float a[][SIZE], b[][SIZE], c[][SIZE];
```

```
{
    int i, j;

    for (i = 0; i < SIZE; i ++) {
        for (j = 0; j < SIZE; j ++) {
            printf("a[%d][%d] = %3.2fb[%d][%d] = %3.2f",
                i, j, a[i][j], i, j, b[i][j]);
            printf("c[%d][%d] = %3.2f\n", i, j,
                c[i][j]);
        }
    }
}
```

Static Scheduling - Pascal Example

```
{ multiply two matrices, store results in third
  matrix, and print results }

program matrix_mul ;

const

SIZE = 9 ;     { (size of matrices)-1 }

type

matrix = array[0..SIZE, 0..SIZE] of real;
integer = longint;

var

a : matrix ;        { first array }
b : matrix ;        { second array }
c : matrix ;        { result array }
nprocs: longint; { number of processes }
ret_val: longint; { return value for m_set_procs }

procedure m_lock;
    cexternal;
procedure m_unlock;
    cexternal;
function m_set_procs(var i : longint) : longint;
    cexternal;
procedure m_pfork(procedure a);
    cexternal;
function m_get_numprocs : longint;
    cexternal;
```

```
function m_get_myid : longint;
    cexternal;
procedure m_kill_procs;
    cexternal;

{ initialize matrix function }

procedure init_matrix ;
var
i, j : integer ;
begin
    for i := 0 to SIZE do
    begin
        for j := 0 to SIZE do
        begin
            a[i, j] := (i + j) ;
            b[i, j] := (i - j) ;
        end;
    end;
end; { init_matrix }

{ matrix multiply function }

procedure matmul ;

var

i, j, k : integer; { local loop indices }
nprocs  : integer; { number of processes }

begin
    nprocs := m_get_numprocs;       { number of processes }
    i := m_get_myid;        { start at Nth iteration }
    while (i <= SIZE) do
    begin
        for j := 0 to SIZE do
        begin
            for k := 0 to SIZE do
                c[i, k] := c[i, k] + a[i, j] * b[j, k];
        end;
        i := i + nprocs;
    end;
end; { matmul}

{ print results procedure }

procedure print_mats ;
var
```

```
i, j : integer; { local loop indices }
begin
    for i := 0 to SIZE do
    begin
        for j := 0 to SIZE do
        begin
            writeln('a[',i,',',j,'] = ',a[i,j],
                'b[',i,',',j,'] = ',b[i,j],'  c[',i,',',
                j,'] = ',c[i, j]);
        end;
    end;
end; {print_mats}

begin { main program starts here}

    writeln('Enter number of processes:');
    readln(nprocs);

    init_matrix;          { initialize data arrays }
    ret_val := m_set_procs(nprocs);   { set # of processes }
    m_pfork(matmul);             { do matrix multiply }
    m_kill_procs;                { terminate child processes }
    print_mats;                  { print results }

end. { main program }
```

Dynamic Scheduling - C Example

```
/* use Cartesian coordinates to find the city closest to
   Beaverton, Oregon, and print the name and distance
   from Beaverton */

#include <stdio.h>
#include <math.h>
#include <parallel/microtask.h> /* microtasking header */
#include <parallel/parallel.h> /* parallel library
                    header */

#define NCITIES 10     /* number of cities */
#define BITE 1         /* bite of work for hungry puppy */

    /* Global shared memory data */

    shared float shortest;    /* distance to
                        nearest city */
    shared int closest;       /* index of
                        nearest city */
```

```
    struct location {
        char *name;
        float x, y;
    };
    shared struct location cities[NCITIES] = {
        { "CHICAGO", 2000., 100. },
        { "DENVER", 500., -550. },
        { "NEW YORK", 150., 100. },
        { "SEATTLE", 0., 200. },
        { "MIAMI", 3500., -2000. },
        { "SAN FRANCISCO", -100., -1000. },
        { "RENO", 200., -600. },
        { "PORTLAND", -17., 0.  },
        { "WASHINGTON D.C.", 3000., -400. },
        { "TILLAMOOK", -70., -50. },
    };
    shared struct location beaverton = { "BEAVERTON",
        0., 0. };

main ()
{
  void get_cities(), find_dis(), m_fork();

  shortest = 999999999.;
  m_fork(find_dis, cities);
  printf("%s is closest to Beaverton.0,
      cities[closest].name);
  printf("%s is %3.2f miles from Beaverton.\n",
      cities[closest].name, shortest);
}
/* find distance to nearest city */

void
find_dis(cities)
struct location cities[];
{
int i, base, top;  /* local loop index, start & end value */
float xsqdis, ysqdis, dist;

while ((base = BITE*(m_next( )-1)) < NCITIES) {
    top = base + BITE;    /* take a bite of work */
    if (top >= NCITIES)
        top = NCITIES-1;

        /* execute all iterations in bite of work */

        for (i = base; i <= top; i++) {
            xsqdis = pow(fabs(beaverton.x - cities[i].x),2.);
```

```
            ysqdis = pow(fabs(beaverton.y - cities[i].y),2.
            dist   = sqrt(xsqdis + ysqdis);
            m_lock();
            if (dist < shortest) {
                closest = i;
                shortest = dist;
                }
            m_unlock();
        }
    }
}
```

Dynamic Scheduling - Pascal Example

```
{ use Cartesian coordinates to find the city closest
  to Beaverton, Oregon, and print the name and
  distance from Beaverton }

program find_distance ;

const

NCITIES = 10;      { number of cities }
BITE = 1;          { bite of work for a hungry puppy }

type

cityrecord =
    record
    name : string [15]; { names of cities }
    x : real;         { x coordinates }
    y : real          { y coordinates }
    end;

var

closest : integer ; { index of nearest city }
shortest : real ;   { distance to nearest city }
cities : array[1..NCITIES] of cityrecord ; { city info }
beaverton : cityrecord ; { coordinates of Beaverton }

procedure m_lock;
    cexternal;
procedure m_unlock;
    cexternal;
procedure m_pfork(procedure a);
    cexternal;
```

```
function m_next : longint;
    cexternal;

{ initialize array of city data }

procedure init_cities ;

begin

    cities[1].name := 'CHICAGO';
    cities[1].x := 2000.0;
    cities[1].y := 100.0;
    cities[2].name := 'DENVER';
    cities[2].x := 500.0;
    cities[2].y := -550.0;
    cities[3].name := 'NEW YORK';
    cities[3].x := 1500.0;
    cities[3].y := 100.0;
    cities[4].name := 'SEATTLE';
    cities[4].x := 0.0;
    cities[4].y := 200.0;
    cities[5].name := 'MIAMI';
    cities[5].x := 3500.0;
    cities[5].y := 2000.0;
    cities[6].name := 'SAN FRANCISCO';
    cities[6].x := -100.0;
    cities[6].y := -1000.0;
    cities[7].name := 'RENO';
    cities[7].x := 200.0;
    cities[7].y := -600.0;
    cities[8].name := 'PORTLAND';
    cities[8].x := -17.0;
    cities[8].y := 0.0;
    cities[9].name := 'WASHINGTON D.C';
    cities[9].x := 3000.0;
    cities[9].y := -400.0;
    cities[10].name := 'TILLAMOOK';
    cities[10].x := -70.0;
    cities[10].y := -50.0;

    beaverton.name := 'BEAVERTON';
    beaverton.x := 0.0;
    beaverton.y := 0.0;

end; { of init_cities }

{ find distance to nearest city }
procedure find_dis;
```

```pascal
var

i, base, top : longint ;   { local index, start value,
                    end value }
xsqdis, ysqdis, dist : real ;

begin
    base := BITE * m_next;
    while (base < NCITIES) do
    begin
        top := base + BITE;
        i := base;
        while (i < top) do
        begin
            xsqdis := sqr(beaverton.x -
                cities[i].x);
            ysqdis := sqr(beaverton.y -
                cities[i].y);
            dist   := sqrt(xsqdis + ysqdis);

            m_lock;
            if (dist < shortest) then
            begin
                closest := i;
                shortest := dist;
            end;
            m_unlock;

            i := i + 1 ;
        end;
    base := BITE * m_next;
    end;
end;

begin { main program starts here }

    shortest := 999999999.0;

    init_cities;
    m_pfork(find_dis);
    writeln(cities[closest].name,
        ' is closest to Beaverton.');
    writeln(cities[closest].name, ' is ', shortest,
        ' miles from Beaverton.');

end.
```

Dynamic Shared Memory Allocation - C Example

```c
/* multiply two matrices, store results in third
   matrix, and print results */

#include <stdio.h>
#include <parallel/microtask.h>
#include <parallel/parallel.h>

     /* Global shared memory data */

        shared float **a; /* first array */
        shared float **b; /* second array */
        shared float **c; /* result array */

main ()
{
  char *shmalloc();
  float ** setup_matrix();
  void init_matrix(), m_fork(), m_kill_procs(),
    matmul(), print_mats();
  int size ; /* loop end value and loop increment */

  printf("Enter array size:");
  scanf("%d",&size);

  a = setup_matrix (size, size);  /* allocate shared */
  b = setup_matrix (size, size);  /* memory */
  c = setup_matrix (size, size);
  init_matrix(a, b, size, size);  /* initialize data */
  m_set_procs(3);                 /* set # of processes */
  m_fork(matmul, a, b, c, size, size); /* execute matmul */
  m_kill_procs();                 /* kill childprocesses */
  print_mats(a, b, c, size, size); /* print results */
}

/* initialize matrix function */

float **
setup_matrix(nrows, ncols)
int nrows, ncols;
{
int i, j;
float **new_matrix;

  /*   allocate pointer arrays : set new_matrix to
       address of newly allocated shared matrix */
```

```
new_matrix = (float**)shmalloc((unsigned)nrows*
    (sizeof(float*))));

  /*  allocate data arrays : set first element of
      new_matrix to address of first element of
      newly allocated data array */

new_matrix[0] = (float*)shmalloc((unsigned)nrows *
                ncols * (sizeof(float)));

  /*  initialize pointer arrays : set each element of
      new_matrix to address of corresponding element
      of data array */

for (i = 1; i < nrows; i++) {
    new_matrix[i] = new_matrix[0] + (ncols * i);
  }
return (new_matrix);
}
/* initialize matrix function */

void
init_matrix(a, b, nrows, ncols)
float **a, **b, **c;
int nrows, ncols;
{
int i, j;

    for (i = 0; i < nrows; i ++) {
        for (j = 0; j < ncols; j ++) {
            a[i][j] = (float)i + j;
            b[i][j] = (float)i - j;
        }
    }
}
void
matmul(a, b, c, nrows, ncols)
float **a, **b, **c;
int nrows, ncols;
{
int i, j, k, nprocs;

nprocs = m_get_numprocs();
    for (i = m_get_myid(); i < nrows; i += nprocs) {
        for (k = 0; k < ncols; k ++) {
            c[i][k] = 0.0;
            for (j = 0; j < ncols; j ++) {
                c[i][k] += a[i][j] * b[j][k];
```

```
               }
           }
       }
}
void
print_mats(a, b, c, nrows, ncols)
float **a, **b, **c;
int nrows, ncols;
{
int i, j;

    for (i = 0; i < nrows; i ++) {
        for (j = 0; j < ncols; j ++) {
            printf("a[%d][%d] = %3.2fb[%d][%d] = %3.2f",
            i, j, a[i][j], i, j, b[i][j]);
            printf("c[%d][%d] = %3.2f\n", i, j, c[i][j]);
        }
    }
}
```

5.6. Compiling, Executing, and Debugging

To complete development of your data-partitioned program, follow these steps:

1.   Invoke the appropriate compiler with the proper options to link your program with the Parallel Programming Library.

2.   Execute the program and check the results.

3.   If necessary, use the DYNIX parallel symbolic debugger, Pdbx, to debug the program.

5.6.1 Compiling the Program

To compile and link a C program, enter the following command:

cc *program.c* **-lpps**

This command compiles a C source file and links the object code with the Parallel Programming Library, producing an executable file named *a.out*. You can also include the **-g** compiler option to create a file of debugging information. (For more information on these options and other C compiler options, refer to the *Sequent C Compiler User's Manual*.)

NOTE

*At some optimization levels, the C optimizer can
remove conditional tests in spin loops. If your codes
uses any spin loop on shared variables, always compile
with the* **-i** *compiler option to ensure that the
conditional tests are preserved. For more information
on the* **-i** *option, refer to* cc(1).

To compile and link a Pascal program, enter the following command:

pascal -mp *program.p*

This command compiles a Pascal source file and links the object code
with the Parallel Programming Library, producing an executable file
named *a.out*. It also places all global variables into shared memory.
You can also include the **-g**, compiler option to create a file of debugging
information. To use the Pdbx debugger on Pascal programs, you will also
need to use the **-o** compiler option to give the executable file the same
base name as the source file. (For more information on these options
and other Pascal compiler options, refer to the *Sequent Pascal Compiler
User's Manual*.)

To compile and link a FORTRAN program, enter the following command:

fortran -F/_shcom_**/** *program.name* **-lpps**

This command compiles a FORTRAN source file and links the object
code with the Parallel Programming Library, producing an executable file
named *a.out*. It also places all COMMON blocks declared with the -F
option into shared memory. (The COMMON block names must start
and end with underbars and be enclosed in slashes (/).) You can also include the **-g** or **-gv** compiler option to create a file of debugging information. To use the Pdbx debugger on FORTRAN programs, you will also
need to use the **-o** compiler option to give the executable file the same
base name as the source file. (For more information on these options
and other FORTRAN compiler options, refer to the *Sequent FORTRAN
Compiler User's Manual*.)

For more information on the DYNIX linker, refer to the *ld(1)* man page
in the *DYNIX Programmer's Manual*.

5.6.2 Executing the Program

To execute the program, simply enter the name of the executable file as a DYNIX command. The default file name is *a.out*.

5.6.3 Debugging the Program

If your program produces incorrect results, you can use the DYNIX Pdbx debugger to isolate any problems. Pdbx is a high-level language symbolic debugger. It is based on dbx, a debugger widely used in UNIX systems.

When using Pdbx to debug programs that use the Parallel Programming library, remember that by default the debugger takes a breakpoint upon exit from child processes. When the debugger encounters these breakpoints, you must enter a Ctrl-Z to return control to Pdbx and continue execution. To disable the automatic breakpoint, use the Pdbx command **ignore exit**.

The Parallel Programming library uses the signal **SIGSEGV** to determine when to allocate more space for a process's shared stack. The debugger automatically stops whenever this signal is encountered. To disable these automatic breakpoints, use the command **ignore sigsegv**. For more information on Pdbx, refer to the *Sequent Pdbx User's Manual*.

5.7. Additional Sources of Information

The following sources provide information that may be helpful to you:

- The *Sequent C Compiler User's Manual* describes in detail the Sequent C language, the compiler, and its options.

- The *Sequent Pascal Compiler User's Manual* describes in detail the Sequent Pascal language, the compiler, and its options.

- The *Sequent FORTRAN Compiler User's Manual* describes in detail the Sequent FORTRAN language, the compiler, and its options.

- The *DYNIX Programmer's Manual* provides more detailed descriptions of the DYNIX Parallel Programming Library routines and the DYNIX linker, ld.

- The *Sequent Pdbx User's Manual* provides instructions for using the Pdbx debugger and reference information on the debugger command set.

- Appendices A and B discuss factors that may affect the execution speed of your program.

- Appendix D contains the DYNIX man pages for the Parallel Programming Library.

- Appendix E lists other literature on parallel programming.

Chapter 6

Function Partitioning on a Sequent System

Page

Illustrations

Fig. No.   Page

Chapter 6

Function Partitioning on a Sequent System

6.1. Introduction

This chapter describes the Sequent system facilities that support function-partitioning applications. These include facilities for:

- Process creation

- Assignment of processing tasks

- Process synchronization

- Interprocess communication

- Ensuring exclusive access to shared data

This chapter also discusses two simple techniques for function partitioning and presents examples showing how to create shared memory for unrelated processes.

6.2. Models for Function Partitioning

Function partitioning involves creating multiple processes and having them perform different operations on the same data set. The processes may be created within a single program or they may be independent programs created at the operating system level. (DYNIX system calls linked by pipes are a good example of function partitioning at the operating system level.) The difference between function partitioning at the program level and simple multiprogramming is that the independent processes *cooperate* to solve a single application.

The methods and applications for function partitioning are much too varied to fully describe here. However, we can present two basic techniques for function partitioning: the fork-join technique and the pipeline technique. By using one or a combination of these models, you can solve any function partitioning application.

6.2.1 The Fork-Join Technique

The fork-join technique is appropriate for applications in which no major function requires the results of any other; that is, each major function must be *independent* of the others. For example, consider an application that computes the mean, the mode, and the median of some set of data. None of these calculations depends on the results of either of the others. This application is a good candidate for the fork-join technique.

The algorithm for a fork-join application is:

1. Create a set of processes, giving each one access to a set of shared data. (This step is the fork.)

2. Assign a task to each process.

3. If there is any data that could be accessed simultaneously by two or more processes, protect it with a lock.

4. As each process finishes its task, it waits at a barrier until the other processes are finished. (This step is the join.)

5. Proceed with serial execution.

Figure 6-1 illustrates the fork-join programming model.

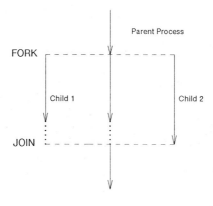

Fig. 6-1. Fork-join function-partitioning model.

6.2.2 The Pipeline Technique

The pipeline technique is appropriate for applications in which the major functions are dependent on each other and the data set or sets are very large. For example, the pipeline technique would be appropriate for a signal-processing application that analyzes satellite data to determine a finite set of categories, assigns each data point to a category, assigns a color value to each data point, and then uses the results to construct a colored image.

The algorithm for a pipelined application is:

1. Create a set of processes, giving each one access to a set of shared data.

2. Assign a task to each process.

3. The first process performs calculations on a portion of the data, writes the results to shared memory, and notifies the next process that the results are available for processing.

4. Add additional processes, giving the first process new data sets and having each subsequent process use the results of the previous process until all the work is done.

5. When work runs out, each process terminates or, if there are other tasks to be done, relinquishes its processor or spins until it is assigned a new task.

6. Proceed with serial execution.

Figure 6-2 illustrates the pipeline programming model.

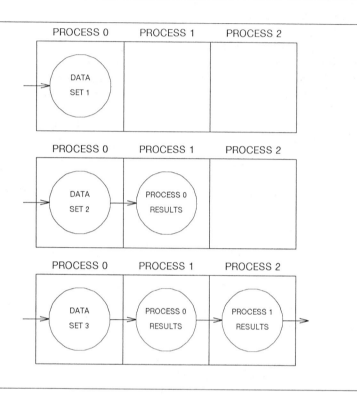

Fig. 6-2. Pipeline function-partitioning model.

6.3. Support for Function Partitioning

The DYNIX operating system provides support for function partitioning with standard UNIX 4.2bsd system calls, with special DYNIX system calls and libraries, and with system calls in the System V Applications Environment.

Since DYNIX supports the UNIX 4.2bsd system call interface, an application can use any of the facilities in UNIX 4.2bsd for process creation, process synchronization, and interprocess communication. Some of these system calls are mentioned here; they are described in detail in Volume 1 of the *DYNIX Programmer's Manual* .

Sequent FORTRAN, Pascal, and C provide intercallability between programs and program modules written in different languages. For more information on intercallability, refer to the *Sequent C Compiler User's Manual*.

The DYNIX Parallel Programming Library contains several routines that can be used for function-partitioning applications. These routines are mentioned here and described in detail in Section 3P of the *DYNIX Programmer's Manual*.

The System V Applications Environment includes a set of system calls for setting up and manipulating message queues and counting, blocking semaphores. These system calls have been added to the standard DYNIX C library, and are transparently available to programs linked in either the "ucb" (default) universe or the "att" universe. Other system calls that are specific to the System V Applications Environment are available only if the System V Applications Environment is installed, and only to programs linked in the "att" universe. See the *DYNIX SVAE Summary* for details. (The programs and code samples shown in this manual are designed to be compiled and linked in the "ucb" universe.)

6.3.1 Process Creation

The `fork()` system call creates a duplicate copy of the current process. In a common type of parallel application on a Sequent system, the parent process sets up a shared memory region and one or more locks, then forks one or more child processes to share the work. The children inherit the parent's complete memory image, including access to shared memory and locks.

The `tmp_ctl()` system call can be used to determine how many processors are in the system and available for use. Your application can use this system call to determine how many processes to create.

6.3.2 Assignment of Processing Tasks

Child processes are identical to the parent. They can be designed to choose their own tasks based on the order of their creation or they can use the `execve()` system call to independently execute new program images. The new image resides in a file that contains either executable object code or a shell script. A child process transformed with an `execve()` never returns to the parent process for new tasks, since the original shared image is destroyed.

6.3.3 Process Synchronization

Synchronization Using the Parallel Programming Library

The Parallel Programming Library routines `s_init_barrier` and `s_wait_barrier` initialize a barrier and cause processes to spin until all related processes arrive at the synchronization point.

Synchronization Using Signals

System calls and library routines such as `sigpause()`, `sigvec()`, `sig block()`, `signal()`, and `kill()` allow processes to send and receive signals among themselves, and to handle special events such as terminal interrupts. On a Sequent system, many synchronization tasks in parallel applications can be performed more easily and efficiently using locks and shared variables. However, these standard system calls are still useful for certain situations.

For example, if a child process determines that the parent will not need any help for a significant amount of time, the child can use `sigpause()` to relinquish its processor for use by other applications. When the parent needs the child, the parent can send the child a wakeup signal using `kill()`.

When using signals, take care to avoid race situations in which processes simultaneously signal each other that they are going to sleep and then all go to sleep, waiting on each other for wakeup signals. If the process expects to be without work for only a few milliseconds, it may be more efficient for the process to spin and do nothing rather than relinquish its processor and then re-acquire one. See Appendix A, "Factors Affecting Performance," for more information on this topic.

UNIX Signals on a Multiprocessor. Because a Sequent system can have multiple processes running simultaneously, some programs that use UNIX signals may behave differently on a Sequent system than on a uniprocessor. For example, suppose process A sends process B a signal. If there is only one processor, A must have it in order to send the signal, and therefore B must be stopped. B is assured of receiving the signal before executing any more user code. On a Sequent system, B may be running (on a different processor) when A sends the signal. If B is running user code, A will send B a software interrupt so that B will enter the kernel and see the signal. However, B will execute some small amount of user code between when A sends the signal and when B receives it.

It is also possible for multiple instances of the same signal from different processes to pile up before the signaled process receives them. In this situation, all but one instance of the signal will be lost. For example, if each of N child processes sends a signal to their parent, the parent will not necessarily receive N signals. This type of race condition is also possible on uniprocessors, but may not manifest itself until the program is ported to a multiprocessor.

Synchronization Using System V Semaphores

The `semop()`, `semget()`, and `semctl()` system calls allow programs to create, acquire, release, and delete counting or blocking semaphores. (Counting semaphores are explained in Chapter 2.) The `semop()` system call supports three basic operations:

1. Acquire (lock) one or more instances of the desired resource (i.e., decrement the semaphore). The process can either wait (block) or return immediately with an error code if the desired resources are not available.

2. Release (unlock) one or more instances of the desired resource (i.e., increment the semaphore).

3. Wait until the semaphore is zero (or return immediately with an error code if it is not).

For specifications of these system calls, refer to the *semop* (2), *semget* (2), and *semctl* (2) entries in AT&T's *UNIX System V Programmer Reference Manual* .

Again, on a Sequent system many process synchronization tasks can be performed more easily and efficiently using locks and shared variables.

6.3.4 Interprocess Communication

Shared Memory

The simplest and most efficient mechanism for interprocess communication is a semaphore in Sequent shared memory. In C programs, shared and private data structures are created by using the `shared` and `private` keywords. In Pascal programs, all global and dynamically allocated data is automatically shared when programs are compiled with the -**mp** compiler option. In FORTRAN programs, common blocks can be designated as shared by using the -**F** linker option, and all static data is automatically shared when the -**mp** option is specified.

NOTE

You can create a private common block within a FOR-TRAN program unit compiled with the **-mp** *option by beginning the common block name with a percent sign (%). For more information, refer to the* Sequent FOR-TRAN Compiler User's Manual.

To map shared files between processes, you can use the DYNIX `mmap()` and `munmap()` system calls. The `mmap()` call maps a portion of a file into a process's virtual address space; `munmap()` cancels the mapping.

The UNIX IPC Facility

The Interprocess Communication (IPC) subsystem of UNIX 4.2bsd provides the ability to transfer data directly between processes using system calls such as `read()` and `write()`. The unidirectional **pipe** facility found in all versions of UNIX is one application of the UNIX 4.2bsd IPC facilities. Other applications use bidirectional data connections or broadcast packets of data to a group of processes. For more information on the IPC facilities, refer to the article "A 4.2BSD Interprocess Communication Primer" in Volume 2 of the *DYNIX Programmer's Manual*, and to man pages such as *socket* (2), *bind* (2), *listen* (2), *connect* (2), and *accept* (2).

On Sequent systems, interprocess communication can often be accomplished more easily and efficiently using shared memory. However, the IPC facilities are extremely useful for certain types of applications, and can be used in situations where shared memory cannot—for example, in applications that may involve processes on different systems.

System V Support

The `msgsnd()`, `msgrcv()`, `msgget()`, and `msgctl()` system calls from the System V Applications Environment provide a mechanism for sending and receiving data between processes via message queues. Data can be packaged in messages of arbitrary length. For specifications of these system calls, refer to the *msgop* (2), *msgget* (2), and *msgctl* (2) entries in AT&T's *UNIX System V Programmer Reference Manual*.

6.3.5 Exclusive Access to Files

Certain applications, such as database management systems, require different processes to take turns reading and writing the same files. The `flock()` system call provides a mechanism for ensuring exclusive access to a file. The `lockf()` (record locking) library routine from the System V Applications Environment can give exclusive access to arbitrary portions of a file. See *s_lock*(3P) or *flock* (2) in the *DYNIX Programmer's Manual* and *lockf*(3C) in AT&T's *UNIX System V Programmer Reference Manual*.

6.4. Additional Sources of Information

The following sources provide information that may be helpful to you:

- The *DYNIX Programmer's Manual* provides more detailed descriptions of the DYNIX Parallel Programming Library routines.

- The *Sequent Pdbx User's Manual* provides instructions for using the Pdbx debugger and reference information on the debugger command set.

- Appendices A and B discuss factors that may affect the execution speed of your program.

- Appendix C includes programming examples showing how to map shared memory between unrelated processes.

- Appendix D contains the DYNIX man pages for the Parallel Programming Library.

- Appendix E lists other literature on parallel programming.

Appendix A

Factors Affecting Performance

Illustrations

Appendix A

Factors Affecting Performance

A.1. Introduction

This appendix provides information to help you estimate the performance improvement you can expect from using a parallel algorithm on a Sequent system. It also provides a variety of figures and guidelines to help you tune your parallel application.

A.2. Maximum Possible Speedup

This section derives a formula, (Amdahl's equation) for determining the maximum possible speedup that can be gained by converting an ordinary sequential program to a parallel algorithm. This formula should be used only as a rule of thumb, since not all the values in this formula can be accurately determined without actually parallelizing the program. Consider the following values:

T   The amount of (wall clock) time the sequential version of the program takes to execute.

N   The number of processors to be dedicated to the parallel version of the program during its execution.

s   The fraction of the execution time T that must be spent in sequential code (e.g., in initialization and I/O). This is usually difficult to estimate accurately, although the **gprof** or **prof** command can be useful in determining what percentage of its time a program spends in each of its subroutines.

For now, assume zero overhead for synchronization and resource contention among the parallel instruction streams. (Figures to help you predict the amount of overhead added by switching to a parallel algorithm are provided in the next section.) Assume that all processors will be kept busy doing useful work for the duration of the parallel sections of the code (i.e., completely effective dynamic load balancing).

The sequential portion of the program will execute in time

$$s \times T$$

and the parallel portion will execute in time

$$\frac{(1-s) \times T}{N}$$

For example, suppose you have a sequential program that takes 100 minutes to execute, 5% of it is sequential code, and you parallelize it over 10 processors. The total execution time for the parallelized version should be in the neighborhood of 15 minutes, a 7X speedup:

$$0.05 \times 100 + \frac{0.95 \times 100}{10} = 14.5$$

Many programs spend less than 1% of their time in sequential code. If we use 1% instead of 5% in our formula, the execution time drops to about 11 minutes, a 9X speedup:

$$0.01 \times 100 + \frac{0.99 \times 100}{10} = 10.9$$

A.3. Processor Availability

Parallel algorithms are simplest and most efficient when they can be based on the following assumption:

> *Every process has a processor whenever it needs to run.*

For example, if you have a 10-processor system, the optimum number of processes for a parallel application is probably 10 or fewer.

In fact, a job that contains more processes than can be kept running simultaneously is likely to encounter the situation illustrated in Figure A-1. Note that the job will eventually run to completion, but possibly at a great cost to system throughput.

Under the scheduling algorithm used by DYNIX, a process will run without interruption on a processor until one of the following events occurs:

- The process blocks (e.g., to wait for an I/O operation to be completed) or terminates.

- The processor is pre-empted by another process with greater or equal priority.

```
Processes 1-9 begin
spinning, waiting for an
event to be posted by
process 10.
                          Process 10 is pre-empted by
                          process 11 and goes to sleep.
Processes 1-9 keep
spinning, consuming
CPU cycles.
                          Process 10 eventually gets a
                          processor, wakes up, and posts
                          the event.
Processes 1-9 resume
productive lives.
```

Fig. A-1. Potential problem due to process/processor mismatch.
If the number of processes in a job exceeds the number of available
processors, the situation illustrated here may be encountered.

Also, the lowest priority process that is running user (non-kernel) code is
required to service all interrupts.

Thus, the problem illustrated in Figure A-1 can be avoided in several
ways:

- Leave one or more processors free to execute other jobs and service interrupts.

- Run the parallel job at a higher priority than other jobs that
  may be running at the same time. (But you will probably want
  to leave one processor free anyway.)

- Use a smarter "wait" algorithm, in which a process blocks after
  spinning for a specified amount of time.

A.4. I/O

I/O in parallel programs is complicated by two factors:

- The need for caution when multiple processes write to the same file

- The tendency for a process to block (relinquish its processor) during an I/O operation

These complications can be reduced by using the following guidelines:

- As much as possible, perform I/O only while a single process is active. If possible, complete all reads before spawning any child processes and delay all writes until after all the children have terminated.

- If it is necessary to perform I/O while multiple processes are active, have one process act as a server to perform all I/O. Use multiple I/O buffers or message buffers, if necessary, to allow the other processes to continue while the I/O server is blocked.

- If all processes must perform I/O, have them write to different files if this is convenient.

- If two or more processes must write to the same sequential file, use the FAPPEND option of the fcntl() system call to ensure that each write occurs at the end of the file.

- If two or more processes must read or write the same direct-access file (i.e., using the lseek() system call followed by read() or write()), place both the lseek() call and the subsequent read() or write() call in the same critical region.

Appendix B

Tuning for Performance

Appendix B

Tuning for Performance

B.1. Introduction

This appendix explains how to tune your Sequent system and your application for maximum execution speed on parallel applications.

B.2. Tuning Virtual Memory and Process Priority

By default, Sequent systems are tuned for optimal system throughput in a multi-user environment, so you may need to do some special tuning for optimal execution speed of a parallel application. The two items that can interfere most with performance of parallel applications are excessive paging due to inadequate resident set size and excessive swapping of parallel processes. The following sections explain how to tune your Sequent system to avoid these problems.

B.2.1 Adjusting Resident Set Size

When a program is executed, the DYNIX system assigns it a resident set size. A process's resident set size determines the amount of text and data it can maintain in physical memory. The resident set size is based on the disk size of the program's image and other factors. The default minimum resident set size is 64 Kbytes. The default maximum resident size is equal to the amount of memory in the system.

Once the resident set size is determined, pages of text and data are brought into memory as needed until the resident set is filled. At that point, one page must be traded out of the resident set for every page that is brought in. The DYNIX system monitors the frequency of these page faults and, if the page fault frequency (pff) is too high, increases the resident set size. If the frequency then becomes too low, the operating system decreases the resident set size. For parallel applications that need periodic access to large data sets, these adjustments can result in periods of frequent page faults and oscillation in the resident set size.

They can also cause delays by trading out pages containing locks, thus delaying processes because the locks are not immediately accessable: they are logically accessable, but they are not physically accessable until a page fault occurs. This is transparent to application programs except for the performance loss.

To avoid these problems, you can adjust your application's virtual memory usage parameters, provided that you are the superuser or that your system is configured to allow other users to make such adjustments. If your system is not configured to allow you to change your virtual memory parameters, you can edit the file */sys/conf/param.c*, set the proper parameters, and use the DYNIX **config** utility to reconfigure the system.

The variables `maxRS` and `maxRSslop` control the maximum resident set size. The boolean variables `root_vm_setrs`, `root_vm_swapable`, and `root_vm_pffable` control whether a non-root process can adjust its own resident set size and page fault frequency. For more information on these parameters and on the **config** utility, refer to the article "Building DYNIX Systems with Config" in the *DYNIX Programmer's Manual*.

Once the system is configured properly, a process can set its own resident set size with **vm_ctl(VM_SETRS)** and impose a per-process limit with **setrlimit(RLIMIT_RES)**. Programs can also use the command prefixes **noswap** and **nopff** to suppress process swapping and adjustment of the process's resident set size based on page fault frequency. For information on how to adjust a program's resident set size, refer to the man pages *vm_ctl(2)* and *getrlimit(2)* in the *DYNIX Programmer's Manual*. For information on the command prefixes, refer to man page *noage(8)*.

B.2.2 Adjusting Process Priority

Another way to ensure optimal performance for a parallel application is to ensure that its processes have higher scheduling priority than standard applications. You can use the **config** utility to configure your system so that a process can set its own priority. The **config** option **root_prio_noage** determines whether a non-root process can prevent itself from aging. Once the system is properly configured, the following system calls can be used to control the scheduling priority of a process:

- **proc_ctl()** — A privileged process can use this system call to keep its effective priority at a specified level, immune to the scheduling heuristics that tend to favor interactive programs.

- **tmp_affinity()** — A privileged process can use this system call to bind itself to a particular processor. The process will not run on any other processor, and has a higher priority on its chosen processor than any non-bound process. This system call can be used to ensure that all processes in an application have uninterrupted use of their processors, and are not preempted by other applications. (However, because of dynamic load balancing on Sequent systems, the same effect can be gained simply by assigning the application a high priority using the **nice** command or **setpriority()** system call, possibly in conjunction with the **proc_ctl** system call.)

Many of the capabilities provided by these system calls can be accessed using the following DYNIX "command prefixes:"

- **noage** — suppress adjustment of the process's priority

- **nice** — adjust the process's priority

- **on** — run the process on the specified processor

For example, the following command line runs the command **grindaway** on processor 1, with aging suppressed and its priority increased by 10 (the lower the **nice** value, the higher the priority):

```
nice -10 on 1 noage grindaway
```

See man pages *nice* (1) and *noage* (8) for details.

B.2.3 Cautions

Overuse of priority and resident set size adjustment can lead to system deadlock. If both **noswap** and **nopff** are specified, you could create a non-swappable process that deadlocks the system by consuming most of physical memory. If both **noage** and **nice** are used, a single program could hang the system by using all the processors and then getting into an infinite loop.

B.3. Hints for Optimization

This section describes some techniques that may help you to further improve the execution speed of your program.

NOTE

> *Benchmark programs present some special tuning problems because they often use large data sets but involve less computation than real applications, so the overhead of paging the data into memory may account for most of the execution time. If you suspect this problem, try executing parallel sections more than once. After the first execution, the data will have been paged into memory, so subsequent repetitions will not have paging overhead.*

B.3.1 Renaming Variables

Renaming variables is a technique that can be used to shorten locked or ordered loop sections, thereby increasing the portion of the loop that can be executed in parallel. To determine whether a loop can benefit from this technique, start at the end of the loop and examine each reference to the locked or ordered variable until you find the last statement where it is assigned a value. If this is not the last reference to the variable, declare a new local variable, assign it the value of the shared locked or shared ordered variable, and substitute the local copy throughout the rest of the loop.

B.3.2 Ensuring Successive Memory References

Unnecessary paging can result when a parallel process must use data scattered among different pages of memory. For best results, try to structure programs so that each parallel process works with a page of data at a time. For matrix operations in FORTRAN programs, you can do this by making each parallel process work with one column of data at a time. For matrix operations in C and Pascal programs, make each process work with one row of data at a time. For FORTRAN DO loops without ordered sections, set the CHUNK parameter as high as possible.

B.3.3 Optimizing Ordered Sections

When executing loops in parallel, the goal is to minimize the amount of code in synchronized sections. In the case of FORTRAN DO loops, this means placing the C$ORDER and C$ENDORDER directives as close together as possible. The following simple rule allows you to minimize ordered DO loop sections: for any two statements, x and y, such that y must be executed after the x statement in a previous loop iteration, the C$ORDER and C$ENDORDER statements must be placed as follows:

- The C$ORDER directive must precede statement y.

- The C$ENDORDER directive must follow statement x.

- The C$ORDER directive must precede the C$ENDORDER directive.

To illustrate how this rule is applied, let's examine the following example loop:

```
      DO 10 i = 2,n
 20   a(i) = c(i) * pi
 30   b(i) = a(i-1) * d(i)
 10   CONTINUE
```

In each iteration of this loop, the value of b(i) depends on the value of a(i) produced in the previous iteration. Applying the rule stated above, the C$ORDER statement must precede statement 30, the C$ENDORDER statement must follow statement 20, and the C$ORDER statement must precede the C$ENDORDER statement. When the directives are inserted according to these rules, the loop looks like this:

```
C$DOACROSS SHARE(a, b, c, d, pi), ORDER(iguard)
      DO 10 i = 2,n
 20   a(i) = c(i) * pi
C$ORDER iguard
C$ENDORDER iguard
 30   b(i) = a(i-1) * d(i)
 10   CONTINUE
```

The ordered section is now very short. In fact, it now encloses no program statements. The C$ORDER directive halts execution of statement 30 of this loop iteration until the C$ENDORDER in the previous iteration is executed. The C$ENDORDER is a signal that statement 20 has been executed and execution of statement 30 can begin for the next loop iteration.

There are two further easy optimizations for ordered sections. First, if an ordered section is nested within another, the inner ordered section requires no C$ORDER and C$ENDORDER statements. Second, if all the ordered sections in a loop are empty (contain no source code statements), then there may be some benefit in splitting the loop into several loops at the ordered sections and placing the loops in order. This loop splitting transforms the single loop into a series of loops with no synchronization. This method is efficient only when the number of processors is very large and the code within the loop is very small. You will have to determine whether the additional loop overhead outweighs the benefits of eliminating ordered sections.

B.4. Tools for Monitoring Performance

B.4.1 The Microsecond Clock

The Sequent microsecond clock allows parallel programmers to do fine-grain timing studies of program execution. All Symmetry systems include a clock. In Balance systems, the clock is an optional board that can be purchased from Sequent and installed on the Multibus.

Users map the clock into process address space with the **usclk_init** library routine and read the clock with the **getusclk** routine. On Symmetry systems, overhead for a **getusclk** call is around 2 microseconds; on Balance systems, overhead is approximately 25 microseconds per call.

For more information on the microsecond clock, refer to *getusclk*(3), *usclk*(4), and *usclk_conf*(8) in the *DYNIX Programmer's Manual*.

B.4.2 The *gprof* Profiler

The DYNIX **gprof** utility creates a program execution profile, a listing that shows you which subprograms (subroutines or functions) account for most of a program's execution time. These subprograms are best to execute in parallel.

In creating a **gprof** listing, you will perform three steps: compiling a C, Pascal, or FORTRAN program with the profiling option, executing the program to produce profile data, and running **gprof** on the profile data. To compile a program for profiling, enter the **fortran, pascal,** or **cc** command with the **-pg** option, as shown in the following examples:

fortran -pg *program.f*

pascal -pg *program.p*

cc -pg *program.c*

(Refer to the *Sequent FORTRAN Compiler User's Manual*, the *Sequent Pascal Compiler User's Manual*, and the *Sequent C Compiler User's Manual* for more information on these compilers.)

Next, execute the compiled program by entering the name of the object file as a command (*a.out* is the default name). After the program executes, profile data is written to a file called *gmon.out*. After execution is complete, enter the following command:

gprof

This command produces an ASCII file named *gmon.sum* which contains the program execution profile. The program profile contains a subprogram list and a set of call graphs. Figure B-1 shows a portion of a subprogram list.

```
%time  cumsecs  seconds     calls  name
 80.1   242.24   242.24    133874  saxpy
  9.2   270.11    27.87        27  matgen
  4.3   283.06    12.95            mcount
  3.4   293.19    10.13        26  sgefa
  1.1   296.64     3.45            %F_MAX
  0.8   299.02     2.38      2574  isamax
  0.6   300.92     1.89      2574  sscal
  0.2   301.48     0.56        26  sgesl
  0.1   301.81     0.33         1  smxpy
  0.0   301.88     0.08         1  noname
```

Fig. B-1. Example subprogram list.

We are concerned with the following information in the subprogram list:

- The leftmost column, %time, gives the percentage of execution time used by each subprogram, including the percentage used by each of its subprograms. The subprograms are listed in descending order according to this percentage.

- The fourth column from the left, `calls`, states the number of calls to the subprogram.

- The last column, `name`, states the name of the subprogram.

From Figure B-1, you can see that the routine `saxpy` is a good candidate for parallel execution, since it accounts for over 80% of the program execution time and is called 133,874 times.

Figure B-2 shows a subprogram call graph.

```
            9.36    0.00     5174/133874       sgesl [6]
          232.88    0.00   128700/133874       sgefa [3]
  [4]  83.7  242.24   0.00   133874           saxpy [4]
```

Fig. B-2. Example subprogram call graph.

We are concerned with the following information in the call graph:

1. The leftmost column contains the index of the call graph. The call graphs cross-reference each other by their index numbers.

2. The second column contains the percentage of the total program execution time accounted for by this subprogram and its descendents (the subprograms that it calls). In Figure B-2, the subprogram accounts for 83.7% of the total execution time.

3. The last column lists the subprogram, its ancestors, and its descendents. The name that stands out to the left is the subprogram that is the subject of the graph; in Figure B-2, the subprogram is `saxpy`. The names listed above this line are the subprogram's ancestors, and the names listed below are its descendent. The square brackets following each subprogram name contain that subprogram's index number.

From Figure B-2 you can see that the routine `saxpy` is called by two routines, `sgefa` and `sgesl`. You will start by looking at these routines and working outwards through the routines in their call graphs until you find the outermost loop, then working back inward through the loops until you find one to execute in parallel.

The information presented here should enable you to use **gprof** to analyze a program for parallel execution. For more detailed information on **gprof**, refer to the DYNIX man page *gprof*(1) or to the article "gprof: A Call Graph Execution Profiler." Both are in the *DYNIX Programmer's Manual*.

B.4.3 The Profiling Library

You can monitor execution of parallel programs that use the Parallel Programming library by linking in the profiling version of the library, *lpps_p.a*. To link this library, you must compile the source files with the -**pg** compiler option and link them with the -**p** option. When the program is run, it produces a file with the suffix *.mon* for the parent process and each child process created by the program. You can then use the *prof* profiling utility to create an execution profile for each process, or you can use the utility's -**s** option to concatenate the *.mon* files and create an execution profile that includes the parent and child processes and all calls to Parallel Programming Library routines.

For more information on the -**pg** and -**p** compiler options, refer to the *Sequent C Compiler User's Manual*, the *Sequent FORTRAN Compiler User's Manual*, or the *Sequent Pascal Compiler User's Manual*. For more information on the *prof* utility, refer to the man page *prof*(1) in the *DYNIX Programmer's Manual*.

Appendix C

Locking Mechanisms and Shared Memory

Illustrations

Appendix C

Locking Mechanisms and Shared Memory

C.1. Introduction

This appendix provides more detail on shared memory and locking mechanisms for readers who are interested in designing their own parallel programming support packages. For more information on Sequent architecture, refer to the *Balance Technical Summary* or the *Symmetry Technical Summary*.

The DYNIX operating system allows two or more processes to share a common region of system memory. Any process with access to a shared memory region can read or write in that region in the same way that it reads or writes in ordinary memory. (The DYNIX support for shared memory is based on the interface proposed in the article "4.2bsd System Manual," a copy of which is found in Volume 2 of the *DYNIX Programmer's Manual*.)

To help ensure that one process does not modify a shared data structure while another process is using it, Sequent systems provide hardware locking mechanisms. On Sequent systems, single-byte load and store operations are always atomic (indivisible), as are 16 and 32-bit loads and stores that are aligned on natural boundaries. To ensure that any other operation is executed atomically, you must protect it with a locking routine using the Balance or Symmetry locking mechanisms.

Balance systems include a set of hardware locks (called Atomic Lock Memory) on each MULTIBUS adapter board. For Symmetry systems, locking is handled by special System Bus and cache protocol. Access to both shared memory and ALM is controlled by the mmap() system call. (See *mmap*(2) for a detailed specification of the mmap() system call.) The locking mechanism in the Symmetry system is invoked with a special prefix to certain Symmetry assembly language instructions.

C.1.1 Balance Systems: Atomic Lock Memory

Mapping Atomic Lock Memory

By default, the only Multibus physical addresses directly accessible to user programs are those associated with ALM. (The superuser can make additional regions of the physical address space, such as those associated with special hardware devices, available using the pmap utility; see *pmap* (4) and *pmap* (8).)

Each MULTIBUS adapter board is assigned 1 Mbyte near the top of the System Bus (physical) address space. Each MULTIBUS adapter's address range is subdivided into several regions, including a 64-Kbyte region for ALM. The 32 2-Kbyte regions of ALM on the first MULTIBUS adapter board are accessed through the special files *alm00* through *alm31* in the */dev/alm* directory. To gain access to an ALM region, a process opens the corresponding file to connect to the **pmap** device driver, then maps it into its virtual address space by using the **mmap( )** system call. Then the process can simply read or write the ALM address space.

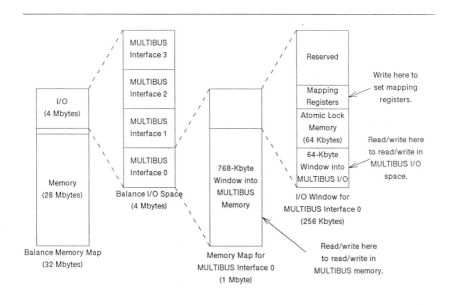

Fig. C-1. ALM in the System Bus address space.

Each 32-bit double-word in the ALM represents one lock, yielding a total of 16K locks per MULTIBUS adapter. Only the least-significant bit of any lock contains useful information. Software must access this bit only through byte operations on double-word boundaries. Any other type of operation causes the system to send a SIGBUS signal to the process.

Lock Operations: Test-and-Set and Clear

A lock's least significant bit determines its state: locked (1) or unlocked (0). Reading a lock returns the state of this bit (0 or 1) and then sets it automatically to 1, thereby locking the lock. This operation is indivisible, or *atomic*. Writing a 0 to a lock location unlocks the lock.

NOTE

On reads from the ALM, bits other than bit 0 are undefined; they must be masked off in software. Reads from bytes other than the least-significant byte set the lock but don't necessarily return the correct lock state. Similarly, writes to bytes other than the least-

significant byte may randomly affect the lock state. Accesses that cross a 32-bit boundary affect two locks simultaneously.

Simple Lock and Unlock Routines

The following code sample illustrates simple routines for locking and unlocking a lock in ALM. The lock() routine simply loops until another process clears the lock to 0. The routine can return at this point, because the hardware relocks the lock (sets it to 1) after reading the 0.

```
/*
 * Lock the ALM lock whose address is lockp.
 */
lock (lockp)
        char     *lockp;
{
        while (*lockp & 1)
                continue;
}


/*
 * Unlock the ALM lock whose address is lockp.
 */
unlock (lockp)
        char     *lockp;
{
        *lockp = 0;
}
```

This implementation works correctly, except that it may place an unnecessary burden on the System Bus. If the ALM lock is locked when the lock() routine is called, lock() repeatedly attempts to read the ALM lock, using System Bus cycles in the process, until the lock is unlocked by another process. (See Figure C-2.) Since accesses to the ALM consume bus bandwidth and compete with accesses to MULTIBUS peripherals, heavy use of this lock() routine may degrade system performance.

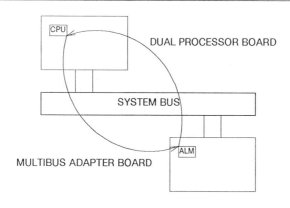

Fig. C-2. Spinning on ALM lock uses System Bus.

Eliminating Unnecessary Bus Usage

An alternative approach is to spin on a *shadow* of the ALM lock—i.e., a copy of the lock in shared memory. Reads from system memory are cached by the dual-processor board. The first time the processor reads from the shadow variable, the block of memory that contains the shadow variable is stored in the processor's cache. Subsequent reads are satisfied by the cache until the processor holding the lock writes a 0 to the shadow variable (i.e., unlocks the lock). When the cache controller sees the write occur, it invalidates the cache block that contains the shadow variable, and the next read returns the new value (0) out of memory. (See Figure C-3.)

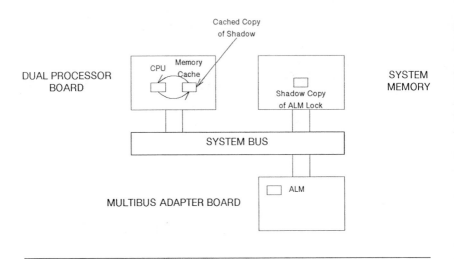

Fig. C-3. Spinning on shadow of lock uses cache.

The following code illustrates lock() and unlock() routines using this technique:

```
struct lock_t {
   char    *lk_alm;        /* address of ALM lock */
   char    lk_shadow;      /* shadow in memory */
};

/*
 * Lock the ALM lock whose address is lockp.
 */
lock (lockp)
        register struct lock_t    *lockp;
{
        /* Go for the ALM lock. */
        while ( *(lockp->lk_alm) & 1) {
                /*
                 * Didn't get it.  Spin until shadow
                 * is unlocked and try again.
                 */
                while (lockp->lk_shadow)
                        continue;
        }
```

```
                    /* Got the ALM lock.  Lock the shadow. */
                    lockp->lk_shadow = 1;
        }

        /*
         * Unlock the ALM lock whose address is lockp.
         */
        unlock (lockp)
                    struct lock_t    *lockp;
        {
                    lockp->lk_shadow = 0;
                    *(lockp->lk_alm) = 0;
        }
```

Multiplexed Locks

Some applications may require more locks than are available in the
hardware. To solve this problem, you can use a single hardware lock to
guard multiple "soft" locks. Each soft lock is a byte in memory with a
value of 1 (locked) or 0 (unlocked). No hardware lock is required to
unlock a soft lock or to spin waiting for it to become unlocked. However,
before locking a soft lock, you must obtain the corresponding hardware
lock to ensure that no other process is locking the soft lock at the same
time. Since the hardware lock is held only while one of its soft locks is
being changed to the locked state, the effect on System Bus traffic is
negligible.

The following code illustrates lock() and unlock() routines for multi-
plexed locks:

```
typedef unsigned char       slock_t; /* 's' for "spin"-lock */

#define  L_UNLOCKED    0
#define  L_LOCKED 1

/*
 * ALM_HASH() is used to hash an address to an ALM offset.
 */

extern   char *_alm_base;        /* virt addr of mapped ALM's */

#define  ALM_HASH(x)  ((int)(&(x)) & (0xFF << 2))
#define  ALM_UNLOCKED 0
#define  ALM_LOCKED    1


/*
```

```
 * lock() provides in-line access to locks for C programs;
 */

#define lock(lp) { \
    register char    *lock_alm = &_alm_base[ALM_HASH(*(lp)]
    for (;;) { \
        /* Wait for lock to be available */ \
        while (*(lp) == L_LOCKED) \
            continue; \
        /* Grab ALM gate for atomic access to lock */ \
        while (*lock_alm & ALM_LOCKED) \
            continue; \
        /* Can race with others trying to get the lock */
        if (*(lp) == L_UNLOCKED) { \
            /* No race (or won it) -- grab the lock */ \
            *(lp) = L_LOCKED; \
            *lock_alm = ALM_UNLOCKED; \
            break; \
        } \
        /* Lost race, try again */ \
        *lock_alm = ALM_UNLOCKED; \
    } \
}

/*
 * unlock() provides in-line unlocking for C programs;
 */
#define unlock(lp)    (*(lp) = L_UNLOCKED)
```

C.1.2 Symmetry Systems: Locked Instructions

The Symmetry locking mechanism is basically the same as the Balance
locking mechanism: bytes of memory are used as locks. The difference is
that Symmetry systems do not require processes to map ALM regions.
Instead, any byte of memory may be used as a lock.

The LOCK Prefix

On Symmetry systems, locking is handled by the System Bus hardware.
Locking mechanisms are therefore implemented in Symmetry assembly
language. These can be included in C programs as asm functions. (For
information on asm functions, refer to the *Sequent C Compiler User's
Manual*.) They can also be implemented as out-of-line locking subroutines such as s_lock and s_unlock.

To set the bus lock, precede an assembly instruction with the LOCK prefix. This prefix assures the atomicity of the instruction that it prefixes. The LOCK prefix can be used with the following assembler instructions for 8, 16, and 32-bit operations: BT, BTS, BTR, BTC, XCHG, ADD, OR, ADC, SBB, AND, SUB, XOR NOT, NEG, and INC. (Refer to the *Symmmetry Series Assembler User's Manual* for more detailed information on these instructions.)

NOTE

The XCHG instruction is always locked, whether it is preceded by the LOCK prefix or not.

Simple Lock and Unlock Routines

Symmetry locking and unlocking routines typically use the XCHG instruction to perform atomic test-and-set and test-and-clear operations. The following example shows one implementation of a locking routine:

```
asm void LOCK(lockadd)
{
%reg lockadd; lab loop, spin, done;

loop: movb  $LOCK, %dl              /* lock byte to register */
      xchgb %dl, (lockadd)          /* atomic test-and-set   */
                                    /* on "soft" lock in mem */
      cmpb  $UNLOCK, %dl            /* if mem location was    */
                                    /* unlocked, we got lock  */
      je    done                    /* we're finished        */
spin: cmpb  $UNLOCK, (lockadd)      /* spin in cache until    */
      je    loop                    /* unlocked, then try     */
      jmp   spin                    /* again for lock        */
done:
}
```

Notice that because this routine uses the XCHG instruction for the atomic test-and-set operation, it does not need the LOCK prefix. Notice also that if the routine's first attempt to set the lock is unsuccessful, it spins in cache while waiting for the lock and does not create additional traffic on the System Bus.

The following example shows one implementation of an unlocking routine:

```
asm void UNLOCK(lockadd)
{
%reg lockadd;

        movb  $UNLOCK, %al    /* unlock byte to register */
        xchgb %al, (lockadd) /* atomic test-and-clear    */
}
```

Again, notice that this routine uses the XCHG instruction for the atomic test-and-set operation, so it does not need the LOCK prefix. When the address of the lock is sent out on the System Bus, any processor spinning in cache and waiting for a lock will see the address on the bus and try again to set the lock.

C.1.3 Shared Memory

The *mmap* (2) entry in Volume 1 of the *DYNIX Programmer's Manual* is a detailed specification of the mmap() system call, upon which the DYNIX shared-memory implementation is based. The following paragraphs examine certain features of mmap() that may be of interest to a programmer writing a parallel programming support package.

Mapping Shared Memory

In general, mmap() can be used to map a portion of any file or any region of the system's physical address space into a process's virtual address space. A process creates a shared-memory region by opening an ordinary file, then using mmap() to map the file into the process's virtual address space. If the high end of the mapped region is above the current program "break" (as returned by the sbrk() system call), the "break" is set to the high end of the mapped region. However, any memory between the old break and the low end of the mapped region is inaccessible (unless it is subsequently mmap-ed).

A shared-memory allocator analogous to malloc() (see *malloc* (3)) can be built using mmap() to acquire needed memory in the same way that malloc() uses sbrk(). In fact, the Parallel Programming Library routines shmalloc(), shbrk(), and shsbrk() use mmap() in this way.

Mapped regions created with mmap() are inherited (i.e., shared) by the process's children. Thus, in an application involving a parent process and one or more identical (not exec-ed) children, the parent first maps the necessary shared-memory and ALM regions, then initializes any locks or other shared variables, then forks the children. (The Parallel Programming Library handles initialization of shared memory and, for Balance systems, ALM by calling the _ppinit( ) routine before calling a program's main( ) routine. This routine maps the program's shared data segment into shared memory, allocates a block of ALM if necessary, and performs miscellaneous run-time initilization for other library routines.) Unrelated processes can also share memory by independently mapping the same file into their virtual memory .

Note, however, that mmap( ) affects only the calling process and any **subsequently** forked children. If child process A expands its shared-memory region, the expansion will not show up in its sibling process, B. If B tries to access a variable set up by A in the new portion of A's address space, B will receive a **SIGSEGV** (segmentation fault) signal. Of course, B can catch this signal and use it as an indication that B needs to grow its own shared-memory region to match A's. This mechanism is used by the Parallel Programming Library to keep all processes' shared-memory regions up to date.

Mapped Files

The Parallel Programming Library immediately unlinks the temporary file that it uses to create the shared memory region. However, there are many ways to use the file that is mapped into a shared memory region:

- The file acts like a paging area for the mapped memory region. The memory contents are copied out to the file when the process is swapped or when it exits, or when the region is otherwise unmapped by the last process that has it mapped. Thus, the file can be useful in post-mortems.

- If the mapped portion of the file already exists when the file is mapped, the contents of the file are immediately available "in memory." (Technically, the contents are paged in as they are needed.) Thus, a previously obtained snapshot of shared memory can be easily restored.

- An application-specific monitor or debugger can plug in to an executing parallel application by mapping the application's mapped file into its own address space.

- Read( ) and write( ) operations to the mapped regions of the file also affect the corresponding memory. Thus, ordinary utilities such as **cp** can be used to capture the contents of shared memory.

Note, however, that a file cannot be truncated while it is mapped. Thus,

```
cp saved_mem mapped_file
```

will not work.

Also note that if you map a file whose size is not an integral multiple of the file system block size (usually 8192), mmap() will pad the file with null bytes to the end of the block. If you do not have write access to the file, mmap() will fail.

Mapping Shared Memory from Unrelated Processes

The following pages contain examples showing how to use the **mmap** system call to create shared memory for unrelated processes. The examples illustrate two techniques. The first, and simplest, technique is to create a single shared file and to use the DYNIX loader, **ld**, to locate the shared data in memory. The second technique is to create multiple shared files and use assembler directives to locate the shared data.

Creating a Single Shared File. Creating a single shared file is a two-part process:

1. Set up a _ppinit subprogram to call **mmap** and initialize shared files. This procedure is automatically called before the main program.

2. Use **ld** to declare the necessary global variable or common block as shared and to declare its location in memory.

The following examples illustrate this process.

NOTE

These examples do not use a full pathname for the shared file, so they must be executed in the same directory.

The following two FORTRAN programs declare the common block SHARED and then take turns writing values to the shared file. The first program, *x1.f*, waits for the other program to write the shared variable A, writes the shared variable B, waits for the other program to write C, then exits.

```
      COMMON /SHARED/ A,B,C
      INTEGER*4 A,B,C

      WRITE(0,1)
    1 FORMAT( 12H WAIT FOR A )

   10 CONTINUE
      IF ( A .EQ. 0 ) GOTO 10

      WRITE(0,2)
    2 FORMAT( 9H WRITE B )

      B = 1

      WRITE(0,3)
    3 FORMAT( 12H WAIT FOR C )

   20 CONTINUE
      IF ( C .EQ. 0 ) GOTO 20

      STOP
      END
```

The second program, *x2.f*, writes the shared variable A, waits for the other program to write the shared variable B, writes the shared variable C, then exits.

```
      COMMON /SHARED/ A,B,C
      INTEGER*4 A,B,C

      WRITE(0,1)
    1 FORMAT( 9H WRITE A )

      A = 1

      WRITE(0,2)
    2 FORMAT( 12H WAIT FOR B )

   10 CONTINUE
      IF ( B .EQ. 0 ) GOTO 10

      WRITE(0,3)
    3 FORMAT( 9H WRITE C )

      C = 1

      STOP
      END
```

The following file, *ppinit.c*, is linked with both FORTRAN programs and is called automatically when the programs are run. This subprogram initializes the shared file and rounds the size of the shared memory segment up to the nearest page boundary:

```
/*
 * _ppinit.c
 *   Parallel program run-time
 *   environment initialization.
 */

#include <a.out.h>
#include <strings.h>
#include <sys/errno.h>
#include <sys/ioctl.h>
#include <sys/types.h>
#include <sys/file.h>
#include <sys/mman.h>

#include <machine/pmap.h>
#include "parc.h"

/*
 * _ppinit()
 *   Parallel startup for C programs.
 *
 */

extern int errno;
int _pgoff;
extern shared char _shstart_, _shend_;


_ppinit()
{
    int fd;
    int szshared;

    fd = open("SHARED_FILE", O_RDWR|O_CREAT, 0666);
    if (fd < 0)
        bad_init("open", errno);

    _pgoff = getpagesize() - 1;

    szshared = (int) PGRND(&_shend_ - &_shstart_);
    if (MMAP(fd, &_shstart_, szshared, 0) < 0)
        bad_init("mmap", errno);
```

```
}


/*
 * bad_init()
 *    For some reason, couldn't init --
 *    complain and exit with error status.
 */

static
bad_init(msg, err)
    char *msg;
    int err;
{
    perror(msg);
    _exit(err);
}
```

The following header file, *parc.h*, defines the MMAP and PGRND macros used in *finit.c*.

```
/*
 * parc.h
 *    Parallel C support library definitions.
 */

/*
 * MMAP() is short-hand for calling mmap().
 */

#define MMAP(fd,va,sz,pos)    \
    mmap(va, sz, PROT_RDWR, MAP_SHARED, fd, pos)
/*
 * PGRND() rounds up a value to next page boundary.
 */

#define PGRND(x)(char *) (((int)(x) + _pgoff) & ~_pgoff)
```

Finally, the following file, *Makefile*, compiles, links, and executes the various sections of this application. Notice that the **fortran** command lines use the loader option **-F** to declare the shared common block and the loader option **-ZO** to declare 10000 as the base address of the shared data segment.

```
all : x1 x2
x1  : x1.f ppinit.o
      fortran -F/SHARED/ -ZO10000 -e -o x1 x1.f finit.o

x2  : x2.f ppinit.o
```

```
                fortran -F/SHARED/ -Z010000 -e -o x2 x2.f finit.

        ppinit.o: ppinit.c

        clean   :
              rm -f x1 x2 *.o SHARED_FILE

        run :
              rm -f SHARED_FILE
              x1 &
              sleep 5
              x2 &
```

Creating Multiple Shared Files. Creating multiple shared files is a three-part process:

1. Set up your main programs to explicitly call a subprogram that initializes shared memory.

2. Set up the subprogram to call **mmap** and initialize shared files.

3. Set up a file of assembler directives that define the starting address of each shared file.

The following examples illustrate this process. (Some of these examples are similar or identical to those in the previous section.)

NOTE

These examples do not use a full pathname for the shared file, so they must be executed in the same directory.

The following two FORTRAN programs declare the common block SHARED, call the subroutine FINIT to initialize shared memory, and then take turns writing values to the shared file. The first program, *x1.f*, waits for the other program to write the shared variable A, writes the shared variable B, waits for the other program to write C, then exits.

```
      COMMON /SHARED/ _START,A,B,C,_END
      INTEGER*4 _START,A,B,C,_END

      EXTERNAL _FINIT

      CALL _FINIT(_START,_END)

      WRITE(0,1)
   1  FORMAT( 12H WAIT FOR A )

  10  CONTINUE
      IF ( A .EQ. 0 ) GOTO 10

      WRITE(0,2)
   2  FORMAT( 9H WRITE B )

      B = 1

      WRITE(0,3)
   3  FORMAT( 12H WAIT FOR C )

  20  CONTINUE
      IF ( C .EQ. 0 ) GOTO 20

      STOP
      END
```

The second program, *x2.f*, initializes itself in the same way as *x1.f*. It then writes the shared variable A, waits for the other program to write the shared variable B, writes the shared variable C, and exits.

```
      COMMON /SHARED/ _START,A,B,C,_END
      INTEGER*4 _START,A,B,C,_END

      EXTERNAL _FINIT

      CALL _FINIT(_START, _END)

      WRITE(0,1)
   1  FORMAT( 9H WRITE A )

      A = 1

      WRITE(0,2)
   2  FORMAT( 12H WAIT FOR B )

  10  CONTINUE
      IF ( B .EQ. 0 ) GOTO 10
```

```
      WRITE( 0,3 )
3     FORMAT( 9H WRITE C )

      C = 1

      STOP
      END
```

The following file, *finit.c*, initializes the shared file and rounds the size of the shared memory segment up to the nearest page boundary:

```
/*
 * finit.c
 *   Parallel program run-time
 *   environment initialization.
 */

#include <a.out.h>
#include <strings.h>
#include <sys/errno.h>
#include <sys/ioctl.h>
#include <sys/types.h>
#include <sys/file.h>
#include <sys/mman.h>

#include <machine/pmap.h>
#include "parc.h"

/*
 * finit()
 *   Parallel startup for C programs.
 *
 */

extern int errno;
int _pgoff;

finit(end, start)
    char *start, *end;
{
    int fd;
    int szshared;

    printf("start %x, end %x0, start, end);
    fd = open("SHARED_FILE", O_RDWR|O_CREAT, 0666);
    if (fd < 0)
        bad_init("open", errno);

    _pgoff = getpagesize() - 1;
```

```
        szshared = (int) PGRND(end - start);
        if (MMAP(fd, start, szshared, 0) < 0)
            bad_init("mmap", errno);
}
/*
 * bad_init()
 *    For some reason, couldn't init --
 *    complain and exit with error status.
 */

static
bad_init(msg, err)
    char *msg;
    int err;
{
    perror(msg);
    _exit(err);
}
```

The following header file, *parc.h*, defines the MMAP and PGRND macros used in *finit.c*.

```
/*
 * parc.h
 *    Parallel C support library definitions.
 */

/*
 * MMAP() is short-hand for calling mmap().
 */

#define MMAP(fd,va,sz,pos)    \
    mmap(va, sz, PROT_RDWR, MAP_SHARED, fd, pos)
/*
 * PGRND() rounds up a value to next page boundary.
 */
#define PGRND(x) (char *) (((int)(x) + _pgoff) & ~_pgoff)
```

The following assembly language file, *x.s*, sets the base address of the SHARED common block:

```
        .globl   /SHARED/
        .set /SHARED/,0x100000
```

Finally, the following file, *Makefile*, compiles, links, and executes the various sections of this application.

```
all       : x1 x2
x1        : x1.f x.o finit.o
              fortran -e -o x1 x1.f x.o finit.o

x2        : x2.f x.o finit.o
              fortran -e -o x2 x2.f x.o finit.o

x.o       : x.s

finit.o      : finit.c

clean     :
          rm -f x1 x2 *.o SHARED_FILE

run       :
          rm -f SHARED_FILE
          x1 & x2 &
```

C.2. Balance Configuration Requirements for ALM

For a program that uses ALM to run on your Balance system, the following conditions must be true. The associated configuration steps must be performed by the superuser.

NOTE

There are no special configuration requirements for Symmetry Systems, since they do not use ALM.

1. The `pmap` pseudo-device driver must be configured into the DYNIX kernel. Verify that your kernel configuration file (e.g., */sys/conf/DYNIX*) contains this line:

    ```
    pseudo-device    pmap              # phys-map driver
    ```

    If this line is not present, you need to add it to the end of your kernel configuration file and rebuild the kernel, as described in the *DYNIX System Administrator's Guide* .

2. The special files *alm00* through *alm31* must reside in the
    /dev/alm directory. If this directory does not exist, enter these
    commands at the system prompt:

    ```
    # cd /dev
    # MAKEDEV alm
    ```

3. The revision number of your MULTIBUS adapter board must
    be 2:1 or greater: earlier revisions do not contain ALM. If you
    execute the **MAKEDEV** alm command and your system does
    not include ALM, **MAKEDEV** will respond as follows:

    ```
    OLD REV MBAD, NO ALM SUPPORT -- CAN'T INSTALL ALM
    DEVICES
    ```

    If your MULTIBUS adapter board has a revision number less
    than 2:1, contact your local sales representative about an up-
    grade.

4. If the MULTIBUS adapter board is not connected to a MUL-
    TIBUS interface board (e.g., you are using the MULTIBUS
    adapter board only for its ALM), the MULTIBUS adapter board
    must be properly jumpered for this configuration.

Appendix D

Parallel Programming Library

This appendix contains the DYNIX man pages for the Parallel Programming Library routines. These man pages are included to give you a better idea of the capabilities and use of the Parallel Programming Library. However, to ensure that you have the most up-to-date information on the library, refer to the man pages in your *DYNIX Programmer's Manual*.

NAME

      intro – introduction to Parallel Programming Library

DESCRIPTION

      These routines constitute the Parallel Programming Library, which supports microtasking and multitasking in C, Pascal, and FORTRAN programs. (For information on microtasking and multitasking programming models, refer to the *Guide to Parallel Programming*.) The Parallel Programming Library is not supported under System V (*att* universe).

      The routines are contained in the file */usr/lib/libpps.a*. These routines are linked into a program by including the **−lpps** option in the **cc** or **ld** command line, or by including the **−lpps** or **−mp** option in the **fortran** or **pascal** command line.

      For an overview of how the Parallel Programming Library routines are used, and for sample programs and related information, refer to the *Guide to Parallel Programming*.

LIST OF FUNCTIONS

      The following routines support microtasking:

Name	Appears on Page	Page Number
m_fork	m_fork.3p	D-7
m_get_myid	m_get_myid.3p	D-9
m_get_numprocs	m_get_numprocs.3p	D-10
m_kill_procs	m_kill_procs.3p	D-11
m_lock	m_lock.3p	D-12
m_multi	m_single.3p	D-17
m_next	m_next.3p	D-13
m_park_procs	m_park_procs.3p	D-14
m_rele_procs	m_park_procs.3p	D-14
m_set_procs	m_set_procs.3p	D-15
m_single	m_single.3p	D-17
m_sync	m_sync.3p	D-19
m_unlock	m_lock.3p	D-12

      The following routines support multitasking:

Name	Appears on Page	Page Number
cpus_online	cpus_online.3p	D-6
s_clock	s_lock.3p	D-20
S_CLOCK	s_lock.3p	D-20
s_init_barrier	s_wait_barrier.3p	D-22
S_INIT_BARRIER	s_wait_barrier.3p	D-22

The following routines support memory allocation for parallel programming. The *brk* and *sbrk* routines are available without loading the Parallel Programming library (see *brk*(2)), but the versions in the Parallel Programming library are necessary for compatibility with the rest of the library.

NAME

brk, sbrk – change private data segment size

SYNOPSIS

C syntax:

#include <parallel/parallel.h>
caddr_t brk(addr)
caddr_t addr;

caddr_t sbrk(incr)
int incr;

Pascal syntax

FORTRAN syntax

DESCRIPTION

These routines are identical to the standard *brk* and *sbrk* (see *brk(2)*) routines except that these routines verify that the private data segment does not overlap the shared data segment which follows it. If the *brk* or *sbrk* call will cause the segments to overlap, the routine issues an error.

ERRORS

If an error occurs, the return value is -1 and the variable *errno* contains the error code. *Brk* and *sbrk* can return the following error codes:

[ENOMEM]   The requested private data segment will overlap the shared data segment.

[ENOMEM]   The routine cannot allocate file system space to expand the file which has been memory mapped to the shared data segment (see *mmap(2)*). The routine tries to allocate file system space from directories in the following order:

1. the directory indicated by the $TMPPATH environmental variable
2. the current directory
3. the user's home directory
4. the directory */usr/tmp*
5. the directory */tmp*

[ENOMEM]   The limit, as set by *setrlimit*, was exceeded.

SEE ALSO

execve(2), getrlimit(2), malloc(3), end(3), vm_ctl(2), *Guide to Parallel Programming*

NOTES

The gap between the private data segment and the shared data segment can be adjusted by using the −**Z** linker option (see *ld*(1)).

When *brk* and *sbrk* increase a program's address space, they also attempt to increase its allowable resident set size (see *vm_ctl*(2)).

NAME

cpus_online – returns the number of CPUs on-line

SYNOPSIS

C syntax

int cpus_online ();

Pascal syntax

function cpus_online : integer;
cexternal;

FORTRAN syntax

integer 4 function cpus_online

DESCRIPTION

The *cpus_online* routine returns the number of processors currently configured and on-line.

SEE ALSO

tmp_ctl(2), *Guide to Parallel Programming*

NAME

m_fork – execute a subprogram in parallel

SYNOPSIS

C syntax:

#include <parallel/microtask.h>
m_fork(func[,arg,...]);
void (func)();
sometype args;

Pascal syntax

function m_pfork: integer;
cexternal;
procedure func(arg,...);
(code)
m_pfork(func[,arg,...]);
args : sometype;

FORTRAN syntax

external func
integer 4 m_fork
i=m_fork(func[,arg,...])
subroutine func(arg,...)

DESCRIPTION

The *m_fork* routine assigns a subprogram to child processes, which then cooperate in executing the subprogram in parallel. The number of child processes used by the *m_fork* call can be set with a previous call to *m_set_procs*. If *m_set_procs* has not been called, the number of child processes defaults to *(number of CPUs on-line) /2*. If the program has no child processes from previous *m_fork* calls, the call creates the child processes. If there are already child processes from a previous call, *m_fork* re-uses the existing processes.

When an *m_fork* call creates child processes, each child process is given a private integer variable called *m_myid*, which identifies it within the set of child processes being created. The parent process's identification number is always zero. The first child process's identification is 1, the second's is 2, and so on. You can call the routine *m_getmyid* to find out the identification number of a child process (see *m_getmyid*(3P)).

For C programs, the header file */parallel/microtask.h* contains an external declaration of the variable *m_myid* and the variable *m_numprocs*, which indicates the total number of processes executing the subprogram (including all the child processes and the parent process).

Once child processes are available, *m_fork* starts them executing the subprogram *func* with the given arguments. (For Pascal programs, *func* must be an inner scope procedure.) The child processes execute the subprogram until they all return from it. At this point, the program returns from the *m_fork* call and the child processes spin, waiting for more work. The program can either kill the child processes with a call to the routine *m_kill*, suspend them with a call to *m_park_procs*, or let the child processes spin until they are re-used by another *m_fork* call. If the child processes are to be re-used, the *m_park_procs* offers the most efficient use of the Sequent system, because it saves the CPU usage of having the processes spin and it saves the overhead of having to recreate processes on the next *m_fork* call.

You must ensure that arguments passed to the subprogram *func* are either "call-by-value" arguments or addresses of data in shared memory. They must not be addresses in the parent's private data segment.

ERRORS

The *m_fork* call fails and no child processes are created if one of the following error conditions occurs:

[EINVAL]   This call to *m_fork* is nested within a previous call.

[EAGAIN]   The *m_fork* call would exceed *nproc*, the system's limit on the total number of executing processes.

[EAGAIN]   The *m_fork* call would exceed *maxuprc*, the system's limit on executing processes for a single user.

NOTES

Each call to *m_fork* resets the global counter (see *m_next*(3P)).

SEE ALSO

getrlimit(2),   shmalloc(3),   brk(3P),   m_set_procs(3P), m_kill_procs(3P), m_next(3P), *Guide to Parallel Programming*

NAME

m_get_myid – return process identification

SYNOPSIS

C syntax:

#include <parallel/microtask.h>
int m_get_myid();
int i;
i=m_get_myid();

Pascal syntax

function m_get_myid : integer ;
cexternal ;

FORTRAN syntax

integer 4 function m_get_myid

DESCRIPTION

The *m_get_myid* routine returns the value of the variable *m_myid*, the process's indentification number. For the parent process, this variable has the value zero. Child processes are assigned identification numbers in the order of their creation: the first child process has identification number 1, the second has 2, and so on. The C header file */usr/include/parallel/microtask.h* contains an external declaration of the variable.

SEE ALSO

fortran(1), m_fork(3P), *Guide to Parallel Programming*

NAME

m_get_numprocs – return number of child processes

SYNOPSIS

C syntax:

#include <parallel/microtask.h>
int m_get_numprocs();

Pascal syntax

function m_get_numprocs : integer ;
cexternal ;

FORTRAN syntax

integer 4 function m_get_numprocs

DESCRIPTION

The *m_get_numprocs* routine returns the value of the variable *m_numprocs*, the current number of processes in the program. This value reflects the number of child processes plus one, the parent process.

SEE ALSO

fortran(1), m_set_procs(3P), *Guide to Parallel Programming*

NAME

m_kill_procs – kill child processes

SYNOPSIS

C syntax:

#include <parallel/microtask.h>
m_kill_procs();

Pascal syntax

procedure m_kill_procs ;
cexternal ;

FORTRAN syntax

subroutine m_kill_procs

DESCRIPTION

The *m_kill_procs* routine terminates the child processes created by a previous call to *m_fork*.

The *m_kill_procs* routine fails if it is called from a subprogram invoked by an *m_fork* call.

ERRORS

The *m_kill_procs* call fails if the following error condition occurs:

[EINVAL]   Some child processes are still executing within an *m_fork* call.

SEE ALSO

m_fork(3P), *Guide to Parallel Programming*

NAME
 m_lock, m_unlock – lock, unlock locks

SYNOPSIS
 C syntax:

 #include <parallel/microtask.h>
 m_lock ();
 m_unlock ();

 Pascal syntax

 procedure m_lock ;
 cexternal ;
 procedure m_unlock ;
 cexternal ;

 FORTRAN syntax

 subroutine m_lock()
 subroutine m_unlock()

DESCRIPTION
 The *m_lock* and *m_unlock* routines are microtasking interfaces to a single *slock_t*-type lock. For a single lock, they are easier to use than the *s_init_lock*, *s_lock*, and *s_unlock* routines because they don't require you to declare or initialize the lock before using it. They are also faster than the other routines because they do not pass the lock address as an argument.

 m_lock locks the lock. *m_lock* is always successful; it spins as long as is necessary to acquire the lock.

 m_unlock unlocks the lock.

SEE ALSO
 intro(3P), s_lock(3P), shmalloc(3P), *Guide to Parallel Programming*

NAME

m_next – increment global counter

SYNOPSIS

C syntax:

#include <parallel/microtask.h>
int m_next();

Pascal syntax

function m_next : longint ;
cexternal ;

FORTRAN syntax

integer 4 function m_next

DESCRIPTION

The *m_next* routine atomically increments a global counter. The program's first call to *m_next* returns the value 1, the second returns 2, and so on. Calls to the *m_fork*, *m_sync*, or *m_single* routines reset the global counter to zero.

SEE ALSO

m_fork(3P), m_sync(3P), m_single(3P), *Guide to Parallel Programming*

NAME

m_park_procs, m_rele_procs – suspend and resume child process execution

SYNOPSIS

C syntax:

#include <parallel/microtask.h>
m_park_procs();
(serial code)
m_rele_procs();

Pascal syntax

procedure m_park_procs ;
cexternal ;
procedure m_rele_procs ;
cexternal ;

FORTRAN syntax

subroutine m_park_procs
subroutine m_rele_procs

DESCRIPTION

The *m_park_procs* routine suspends execution of child processes created by an *m_fork* call. Typically, you would suspend child processes while the parent process is doing extensive I/O or setting up another phase of the program. The *m_rele_procs* routine resumes child process execution when the child processes are again required.

Do not call *m_park_procs* when *m_fork* is executing. Likewise, do not call *m_park_procs* when the child processes are already suspended. To suspend child process execution within an *m_fork* call, use *m_single* and *m_next*.

ERRORS

These routines can return the following error:

[EINVAL] The routine was called in an inappropriate context. For example, the routine was called from a subprogram executing in an *m_fork* call, or the processes were already suspended.

SEE ALSO

m_single(3P), *Guide to Parallel Programming*

NAME

m_set_procs – set number of child processes

SYNOPSIS

C syntax:

#include <parallel/microtask.h>
int m_set_procs(nprocs);
int nprocs;

Pascal syntax

function m_set_procs (var numprocs : longint) : longint;
cexternal;

FORTRAN syntax

integer 4 function m_set_procs(nprocs)
integer 4 nprocs

DESCRIPTION

The *m_set_procs* routine declares the number of processes to execute subprograms in parallel on subsequent calls to *m_fork*. The argument *nprocs* declares the total number of processes that will run in parallel, including the parent process and the child processes. If *nprocs* is zero, the program creates no child processes, but all barriers and locks are initialized as if the program were going to create child processes.

The *m_set_procs* routine initializes a shared variable called *m_numprocs*, which controls the number of processes created by subsequent calls to *m_fork*. The C header file */usr/include/parallel/microtask.h* contains an external declaration of *m_numprocs*, as well as the constant *MAXPROCS* which determines the maximum number of processes that the system will allow the program to create. The other limiting factor is the number of CPUs on-line: *m_nprocs* can be no more than the number of CPUs on-line minus one.

The *m_set_procs* routine is optional: if the program does not call this routine before calling *m_fork*, the number of processes defaults to *(number of CPUs on-line)/2*. The program must not call *m_set_procs* while the child processes from an *m_fork* call are still alive (that is, before an *m_kill_procs* call to kill the child processes).

ERRORS

If an *m_set_procs* call is successful, the return value is zero. If the call fails, the return value is -1 and the variable *errno* holds the error code.

The *m_set_procs* call fails if one of the following error conditions occurs:

[EINVAL]   The argument *nprocs* is greater than MAX-PROCS or it is greater than or equal to the number of on-line CPUs.

[EINVAL]   Children from an *m_fork* call are already running. In this case, call *m_kill_procs* to kill the existing child processes before calling *m_set_procs*.

SEE ALSO

m_fork(3P), m_kill_procs(3P), *Guide to Parallel Programming*

NAME
  m_single, m_multi – mark single-process code section

SYNOPSIS
  C syntax:

  #include <parallel/microtask.h>
  m_single();
  (CODE)
  m_multi();

  Pascal syntax

  procedure m_single;
  cexternal;
  procedure m_multi;
  cexternal;

  FORTRAN syntax

  subroutine m_single
  subroutine m_multi

DESCRIPTION
  The *m_single* routine causes child processes to spin at a barrier
  until the parent process has executed the code following the
  m_single call and called the *m_multi* routine. The child processes
  then resume execution at the source line after the *m_multi* call.
  These routines are typically used to allow the parent process to
  perform I/O or other serial operations during an m_fork call.

NOTES
  Calls to *m_single* are allowed only during *m_fork* calls. To
  suspend child processes after an *m_fork* call, use *m_park_procs*
  and *m_rele_procs*.

  Do not call *m_multi* without calling *m_single first*.

  Nested *m_single* calls are not allowed. Neither are *m_single* calls
  nested between calls to other lock routines, such as *s_lock* and
  s_unlock.

ERRORS
  These routines can return the following error:

  [EINVAL]   The routine was called in an inappropriate con-
                text. For example, *m_fork* had never been called,
                or the processes were already suspended with a
                call to *m_park_procs*.

SEE ALSO

m_park_procs(3P), *Guide to Parallel Programming*

NAME

m_sync − check in at barrier

SYNOPSIS

C syntax:

#include <parallel/microtask.h>
m_sync();

Pascal syntax

procedure m_sync;
cexternal;

FORTRAN syntax

subroutine m_sync

DESCRIPTION

The *m_sync* routine causes a process to spin until all cooperating
processes have reached the same point and called *m_sync*. The
program must not call the *m_sync* routine unless there are multiple
processes executing; that is, unless the program is executing a subprogram during an *m_fork* call and is not between a pair of
m_single/m_multi, *m_lock/m_unlock*, or *s_lock/s_unlock* calls.

NOTES

Calls to *m_sync* reset the global counter (see *m_next*).

ERRORS

These routines can return the following error:

[EINVAL]   There are no child processes executing.

SEE ALSO

m_set_procs(3P), m_fork(3P), m_single(3P), m_park_procs(3P),
m_kill_procs(3P), m_next(3P), *Guide to Parallel Programming*

NAME

s_init_lock, s_lock, s_clock, s_unlock – initialize, lock, unlock locks

SYNOPSIS

C syntax:

#include <parallel/parallel.h>
slock_t lp;
s_init_lock (lp);
S_INIT_LOCK (lp);
s_lock (lp);
S_LOCK (lp);
s_clock (lp);
S_CLOCK (lp);
s_unlock (lp);
S_UNLOCK (lp);

Pascal syntax

procedure s_init_lock(var lp : integer);
cexternal;
procedure s_lock(var lp : integer);
cexternal;
function s_clock : longint;
cexternal;
procedure s_unlock(var lp : integer);
cexternal;

FORTRAN syntax

subroutine s_init_lock(lp)
subroutine s_lock(lp)
subroutine s_clock(lp)
subroutine s_unlock(lp)
integer 1 lp

DESCRIPTION

S_init_lock initializes a memory-based lock. After the lock is initialized, it can be locked with the *s_lock* or *s_clock* routine and unlocked with the *s_unlock* routine. There is no practical limit to the number of locks that can be used by a process.

In the C language, a lock is a shared data structure of type slock_t, as shown in the following declaration statement:

shared slock_t lock;

In Pascal, a lock is a global integer variable. In FORTRAN, a lock is an INTEGER 1 variable. A FORTRAN lock must be placed in shared memory either by declaring it in a common block and using the loader **−F** option or by using the FORTRAN compiler **−mp** option, which places all variables into shared memory.

s_lock and *s_clock* lock the lock whose address is *lp*. The lock must previously have been initialized using *s_init_lock*. *s_lock* is always successful; it spins as long as is necessary to acquire the lock. *s_clock* is successful only if the lock is free; if the lock is held by another process, *s_clock* returns the value L_FAILED. *s_clock* can be used when a process does not need to acquire a particular lock (for instance, when another lock could be used instead).

s_unlock unlocks the lock whose address is *lp*.

S_INIT_LOCK, S_LOCK, S_UNLOCK, and *S_CLOCK* are C-preprocessor macros. (The *S_CLOCK* macro is actually compiled out of line on Balance systems, but it is available for code compatibility.) These macros are found in the header file */usr/include/parallel/parallel.h*. The macros are faster than the normal function calls, but they can add to the code size. See the source code in <parallel/parallel.h> for more information on the macros.

SEE ALSO

intro(3P), shmalloc(3P), fortran(1), ld(1), *Guide to Parallel Programming*

NOTES

The function names *s_init_lock, s_lock, s_clock,* and *s_unlock* are used in C, Pascal, and FORTRAN. In C, the *lp* argument is passed as a pointer to the lock, while in Pascal and FORTRAN, the argument is the address of the lock itself.

NAME
s_init_barrier, s_wait_barrier – initialize barrier, wait at barrier

SYNOPSIS
C syntax:

#include <parallel/parallel.h>
s_init_barrier (bp, nprocs);
sbarrier_t bp;
int nprocs;

S_INIT_BARRIER (bp, nprocs);

s_wait_barrier (bp);
sbarrier_t bp;

S_WAIT_BARRIER (bp);

Pascal syntax

procedure s_init_barrier (var barrier : longint; nprocs : longint);
cexternal;
procedure s_wait_barrier (var barrier : longint);
cexternal;

FORTRAN syntax

integer 4 barrier, nprocs
subroutine s_init_barrier (barrier, nprocs)
subroutine s_wait_barrier (barrier)

DESCRIPTION
S_init_barrier initializes a barrier as a rendezvous point for exactly *nprocs* processes. This barrier can be used subsequently with *s_wait_barrier* .

In C, a barrier is a shared data structure of type sbarrier_t as shown in the following declaration statement:

shared sbarrier_t barrier;

In Pascal, a barrier is a global integer variable. In FORTRAN, a barrier is an INTEGER 4 variable. A FORTRAN barrier must be placed in shared memory either by declaring it in a common block and using the loader **−F** option or by using the FORTRAN **−mp** option, which places all variables into shared memory.

s_wait_barrier delays the process in a busy wait until exactly *nprocs* processes have called *s_wait_barrier*. At that point, all processes exit the busy wait simultaneously. The barrier must have been previously initialized using *s_init_barrier* .

Results are undefined if more than *nprocs* processes call *s_wait_barrier*. A barrier can be used any number of times without being re-initialized. A barrier should not be re-initialized while processes are waiting at the barrier.

S_INIT_BARRIER and *S_WAIT_BARRIER* are C-preprocessor macros. (These macros are actually compiled out of line on Balance systems, but they are available for code compatibility.) These macros are found in the header file */usr/include/parallel/parallel.h*. When compiled in line, the macros are faster than the normal function calls, but they can add to the code size. See the source code in <parallel/parallel.h> for more information on the macros.

SEE ALSO

intro(3P), shmalloc(3P), *Guide to Parallel Programming*

NAME

shbrk, shsbrk − change shared data segment size

SYNOPSIS

C syntax:

#include <parallel/parallel.h>
caddr_t shbrk(addr)
caddr_t addr;

caddr_t shsbrk(incr)
int incr;

Pascal syntax

FORTRAN syntax

DESCRIPTION

For a set of parallel processes executing a single application, *shbrk* sets the system's idea of the lowest shared data segment location not used by the program (called the "shared break") to *addr* (rounded up to the next multiple of the system's page size). Locations greater than *addr* and below the stack pointer or another memory mapped region (see *mmap*(2)) are not in the address space and will thus cause a memory violation if accessed.

In the alternate function, *shsbrk*, *incr* more bytes are added to the program's shared data space and a pointer to the start of the new area is returned.

When a program begins execution via *execve*, the shared break is set at the highest location defined by the program. Ordinarily, therefore, only programs with growing shared data areas need to use *shsbrk*.

When *shbrk* and *shsbrk* increase a program's address space, they also attempt to increase its allowable resident set size (see *vm_ctl*(2)).

RETURN VALUE

Zero is returned if the shared break could be set; −1 if the program requests more memory than the system limit. *shsbrk* returns −1 if the break could not be set.

ERRORS

shbrk and *shsbrk* will fail and no additional memory will be allocated if any of the following error conditions occur:

[EINVAL]   The shared break address would be lowered.

[ENOMEM]   The routine cannot allocate file system space to
                 expand the file which has been memory mapped
                 to the shared data segment (see *mmap*(2)). The
                 routine tries to allocate file system space from
                 directories in the following order:

                 1. the directory indicated by the $TMPPATH
                 environmental variable
                 2. the current directory
                 3. the user's home directory
                 4. the directory */usr/tmp*
                 5. the directory */tmp*

[ENOMEM]   The limit, as set by *setrlimit*, was exceeded.

[ENOMEM]   The new shared data segment would overlap the
                 stack segment.

SEE ALSO

execve(2), getrlimit(2), shmalloc(3), end(3), vm_ctl(2), mmap(2),
Guide to Parallel Programming

BUGS

At this time, the size of the shared data segment can only be
increased.

The shared break cannot be set above the stack segment limit for
any of the processes in the program. (Remember that each process can have a different stack size.) If a process sets the shared
break above the bottom of any process's stack, any reference to
the overlapping area of that stack causes a core dump and aborts
the program with a status of SIGSEGV.

shbrk and *shsbrk* use the SIGSEGV signal and signal handler for
internal purposes. Users who declare their own SIGSEGV
handler cannot expect reliable results from these routines.

If a *shbrk* or *shsbrk* call causes the shared data segment to overlap
a memory mapped region, the shared data segment replaces the
mapped region.

NAME

shmalloc, shrealloc, shfree – shared memory allocator

SYNOPSIS

C syntax:

char   shmalloc(size)
unsigned size;
shfree(ptr)
char   ptr;

char   shrealloc(prt,size)
char   ptr;
unsigned size;

Pascal syntax

FORTRAN syntax

DESCRIPTION

shmalloc, shrealloc, and *shfree* provide a simple general-purpose shared memory allocation package for a set of processes executing a single application. To use these routines, the program must have been linked with the Parallel Programming Library. *shmalloc* returns a pointer to a block of at least *size* bytes beginning on a 4-byte word boundary.

The argument to *shfree* is a pointer to a block previously allocated by *shmalloc;* this space is made available for further allocation, but its contents are left undisturbed.

Clearly, grave disorder will result if the space assigned by *shmalloc* is overrun or if some random number is handed to *shfree*.

shmalloc maintains multiple lists of free blocks according to size, allocating space from the appropriate list. It calls *shsbrk* (see *shbrk*(3P)) to get more memory from the system when there is no suitable space already free. *shmalloc* and *shfree* coordinate the allocation of shared memory among the processes in the task. They maintain a consistent list of free blocks even when several processes are allocating shared memory concurrently. Concurrent requests for shared memory blocks always return unique blocks from the program's shared data segment.

shrealloc changes the size of the block pointed to by *ptr* to *size* bytes and returns a pointer to the (possibly moved) block. The contents will be unchanged up to the lesser of the new and old sizes. If *ptr* points to a freed block, shrealloc returns NULL.

When any of these allocation routines increases a program's address space, it also attempts to increase its allowable resident set size (see *vm_ctl*(2)).

DIAGNOSTICS

shmalloc returns a null pointer (0) if there is no available shared memory or if the region has been detectably corrupted by storing data outside the bounds of a block. *shmalloc* may be recompiled to check the arena very stringently on every transaction; those sites with a source code license may check the source code to see how this can be done.

SEE ALSO

shbrk(3P), vm_ctl(2), *Guide to Parallel Programming*

Appendix E

Bibliography

The area of parallel programming is extremely well published. An attempt to create a thorough bibliography of the subject is well beyond the scope of this document. Therefore, the following sections provide a sampling of literature on parallel programming, parallel programming languages, and parallel programming algorithms and methods. Many of the works listed here contain extensive bibliographies, which should enable you to find further information on topics of special interest to you.

General Topics in Parallel Programming

1. Baer, J.L. "A Survey of Some Theoretical Aspects of Multiprocessing." *Computing Surveys* Vol. 5 No. 1, March 1973, pp. 31-80.

2. Beck, R., and D. M. Olien. "A Parallel Programming Process Model" *Conference Proceedings* Winter USENIX 1987.

3. Bowen, B.A. and R.J.A. Buhr. *The Logical Design of Multiple-Microprocessor Systems.* Englewood Cliffs, N.J.: Prentice-Hall, Inc., 1980.

4. Gelernter, D. "Domesticating Parallelism." *Computer* Vol. 19, No. 8, August 1986, pp.12-16.

5. Gonzalez, M.J. and C.V. Ramamoorthy. "Parallel Task Execution in a Decentralized System." *IEEE Transactions on Computers* Vol. 21 No. 12, December 1972, pp. 1310-1322.

6. Hudak, P. "Para-Functional Programming." *Computer* Vol. 19, No. 8, August 1986, pp.61-71.

7. Kowalik, J.S., ed. *Parallel MIMD Computation: The HEP Supercomputer and Its Applications.* Cambridge, Mass.: MIT Press, 1985.

8. Kuck, D.J. "A Survey of Parallel Machine Organization and Programming." *Computing Surveys* Vol. 9 No. 1, March 1977, pp. 29-59.

9. Lampson, B.W., M. Paul, and H.J. Siegert, eds. *Distributed Systems - Architecture and Implementation* in Goos, G. and J. Hartmanis, eds. *Lecture Notes in Computer Science* Berlin and Heidelberg, W. Germany: Springer-Verlag, 1981.

10. Lorin, H. *Parallelism in Hardware and Software: Real and Apparent Concurrency.* Englewood Cliffs, N.J.: Prentice-Hall, Inc., 1972.

11. Shani, S. "Scheduling Multipipeline and Multiprocessor Computers." *IEEE Transactions on Computers* Vol. 33 No. 7, July, 1984, pp. 637-645.

Parallel Programming Languages

1. Appelbe, W.F. and C.E. McDowell. "High-level Language Primitives for Parallel Algorithms." Internal Report, Electrical Engineering and Computer Science Dept. C-014, University of California, San Diego, March 1985.

2. Brooks, E.D. "A Multitasking Kernel for the C and FORTRAN Programming Languages." *Technical Report UCID-20167*, Lawrence Livermore National Laboratory, September 1984.

3. Gehani, A. H., and W. D. Roome. "Concurrent C -- An Overview" *Conference Proceedings* Winter USENIX 1985.

4. Gehani, N. *Ada Concurrent Programming.* Englewood Cliffs, N.J.: Prentice-Hall, Inc., 1984. [Gehani 1984]

5. Halstead, R. and J. Loaiza. "Multilisp: A Language for Concurrent Symbolic Computation." *ACM Transactions on Programming Languages and Systems* October 1985.

6. Hansen, P. B. *The Architecture of Concurrent Programs.* Englewood Cliffs, N.J. : Prentice-Hall, Inc., 1977.

7. Mundie, D.A. and D.A. Fischer. "Parallel Processing in Ada." *Computer* Vol. 19, No. 8, August 1986, pp. 20-25.

8. Olien, D.M. "Parallel Ada Tasking on the Balance 8000." *Proceedings* Winter UNIFORUM 1987.

9. Padua, D.A., D.J. Kuck, and D.H. Lawrie. "High-Speed Multiprocessors and Compilation Techniques." *IEEE Transactions on Computers* Vol. 29 No. 9, September 1980, pp. 763-776.

10. Schwetman, H. "PPL: Parallel Programming Language." *MCC Technical Report PP-096-86* Microelectronics and Computer Technology Corp., Austin, Tx., February 1986.

11. Shapiro, E. "A Subset of Concurrent Prolog and Its Interpreter." *ICOT Technical Report TR-003*, February 1983.

12. United States Department of Defense. *Reference Manual for the Ada Programming Language.* ANSI/MIL-STD-1815A-1983, February 1983.

Algorithms and Programming Techniques

1. Andrews, G., and F. Schneider. "Concepts and Notations for Concurrent Programming." *ACM Computing Surveys* Vol. 15 No. 1, March 1983, pp. 3-44.

2. Banerjee, U., S.C. Shen, D.J. Kuck, and R.A. Towle. "Time and Parallel Processor Bounds for FORTRAN-like Loops." *IEEE Transactions on Computers* Vol. 28 No. 9, September 1979, pp. 660-670.

3. Banerjee, U., and D.D. Gajski. "Fast Execution of Loops with IF Statements." *IEEE Transactions on Computers* Vol. 33 No. 11, November 1984, pp. 1030-1033.

4. Bernstein, A.J. "Analysis of Programs for Parallel Processing." *IEEE Transactions on Electronic Computers* Vol. 15 No. 5, October 1966, pp. 757-763.

5. Cray Research, Inc. "Multitasking User Guide" *Cray Computer Systems Technical Note SN-0222* Mendota Heights, Minn. : Cray Research, Inc., 1984.

6. Cytron, R. "Useful Parallelism in a Multiprocessing Environment." *Proceedings of the International Conference on Parallel Processing* Washington, D.C. : IEEE Computer Society Press, 1985. pp. 450-457.

7. Gajski, D.D. "An Algorithm for Solving Linear Recurrence Systems on Parallel and Pipelined Machines." *IEEE Transactions on Computers* Vol. 30 No. 3, March 1981, pp. 190-206.

8. Hansen, P. B. "Concurrent Programming Concepts." *ACM Computing Surveys* Vol. 5 No. 4, December 1973, pp. 223-245.

9. Hoare, C.A.R. "Communicating Sequential Processes." *Proceedings of the ACM* Vol. 21 No. 11, August 1978, pp. 666-667.

10. Jordan, H.F., M.S. Benten, and N.S. Arenstorf. *Force User's Manual.* Computer Systems Design Group, Department of Electrical and Computer Engineering, University of Colorado at Boulder, October 1986.

11. Kasahara, H. and S. Narita. "Practical Multiprocessor Scheduling Algorithms for Efficient Parallel Processing." *IEEE Transactions on Computers* Vol. 33 No. 11, November 1984, pp. 1023-1029.

12. Kennedy, K. and D. Callahan. "Analysis of Interprocedural Side Effects in a Parallel Programming Environment" Department of Computer Science, Rice University, Houston, Texas May 1987.

13. Knuth, D. "An Empirical Study of FORTRAN Programs." *Software Practice and Experience* Vol. 1, 1971, pp. 105-133.

14. Kuck, D.J., Y. Muraoka, and S.C. Chen. "On the Number of Operations Simultaneously Executable in FORTRAN-like Programs and Their Resulting Speed-up." *IEEE Transactions on Computers* Vol. 21 No. 12, December 1972, pp. 1293-1310.

15. Lusk, E.L., R. Olson, and R.A. Overbeek. "A Tutorial on the Use of Monitors in C: Writing Portable Code for Multiprocessors" Mathematics and Computer Science Division, Argonne National Laboratory, Argonne, Ill., 1986.

16. Maruyama, K. "On the Parallel Evaluation of Polynomials." *IEEE Transactions on Computers* Vol. 22 No. 1, January 1973, pp. 2-5.

17. Mehrotra, R. and E.F. Gehringer. "Superlinear Speedup Through Randomized Algorithms." *Proceedings of the International Conference on Parallel Processing* Washington, D.C. : IEEE Computer Society Press, 1985. pp. 291-300.

18. Muchnick, S.S. and N.D. Jones, eds. *Program Flow Analysis: Theory and Applications.* Englewood Cliffs, N.J.: Prentice-Hall, Inc., 1981.

19. Padua, D.A. and M.J. Wolfe. "Advanced Compiler Optimization for Supercomputers." *Communications of the ACM* Vol. 29, No. 12, December 1986, pp. 1184-1201.

20. Paige, R.C. and C.P. Kruskal. "Parallel Algorithms for Shortest Path Problems." *Proceedings of the International Conference on Parallel Processing* Washington, D.C. : IEEE Computer Society Press, 1985. pp. 14-19.

21. Ramamoorthy, C.V. and M.J. Gonzalez. "A Survey of the Techniques for Recognizing Parallel Processable Streams in Computer Programs." *AFIPS Conference Proceedings, 1969 Fall Joint Computer Conference* Montvale, N.J.: AFIPS Press, 1969, pp. 1-15.

22. Riseman, E.M. and C.C. Foster. "The Inhibition of Potential Parallelism by Conditional Jumps." *IEEE Transactions on Computers* Vol. 21 No. 12, December 1972, pp. 1405-1411.

23. Rudolph, L. and W. Steiger. "Subset Selection in Parallel." *Proceedings of the International Conference on Parallel Processing* Washington, D.C. : IEEE Computer Society Press, 1985, pp. 11-13.

24. Tenorio, M.F.M. and D.I. Moldovan. "Mapping Production Systems into Multiprocessors." *Proceedings of the International Conference on Parallel Processing* Washington, D.C. : IEEE Computer Society Press, 1985, pp. 56-62.

25. Tjaden, G.S. and M.J. Flynn. "Detection and Parallel Execution of Independent Instructions." *IEEE Transactions on Computers* Vol. 19 No. 10, October 1970, pp. 889-895.

26. Wei, M.C. and H.A. Sholl. "An Expression Model for Extraction and Evaluation of Parallelism in Control Structures." *IEEE Transactions on Computers* Vol. 31 No. 9, September 1982, pp. 851-863.

27. Wolfe, M.J. "Techniques for Improving the Inherent Parallelism in Programs." *Technical Report UIUCDCS-R-78-929, Department of Computer Science, University of Illinois,* July 1978.

Glossary

barrier. A synchronization point. All processes wait at the barrier until the last process arrives, at which time all processes proceed.

blocking. Releasing a processor for use by other processes. Processes can choose to block, rather than spin, during long periods of inactivity.

critical section. A program section that can yield incorrect results if two or more processes try to execute the section at the same time.

data partitioning. A programming method that involves creating multiple, identical processes, each of which performs the same operations on a different portion of the program data.

dependent loop. A loop in which the operations in each iteration depend on the results of previous iterations.

dynamic scheduling. A scheduling method that allows processes to schedule their own tasks through a shared task queue or shared counter.

DYNIX. "DYnamic UNIX," the operating system of Sequent systems. DYNIX is a version of UNIX 4.2bsd that has been modified to support both software-transparent multiprocessing and explicit parallel programming.

event. Something that must happen before a task or process can proceed.

fork. A DYNIX system call that creates a new process that is identical to the calling process. The calling process is called the "parent", and the new process is called the "child".

function partitioning. A programming method that involves creating multiple processes (usually running different programs) and having them perform different operations on a shared data set.

heap. The portion of a program's data area that is allocated at run time.

heterogeneous multitasking. See **function partitioning**.

homogeneous multitasking. See **data partitioning**.

independent loop. A loop that passes no information between loop iterations other than the value of the loop index.

lock. A semaphore which ensures that only one process at a time can access a shared data structure or execute a critical region of code.

microtasking. A data-partitioning method that automatically divides the computing load according to the number of available processes.

multiprogramming. An operating system feature that allows a computer to execute multiple unrelated programs concurrently.

multitasking. A programming technique that allows a single application to consist of multiple processes executing tasks concurrently.

ordered critical section. A point in a program where a task depends on the results of a previous task and execution cannot proceed until the previous task is finished.

overhead. Time and computation not spent in calculating the result of a program. Some examples of overhead are data initialization, I/O, and synchronization.

private data. Data that is accessible by only one process.

process. An instruction stream. Different processes may be instances of the same program, as when the **vi** editor is used by several people simultaneously. Because of DYNIX's dynamic load balancing, a process may migrate from one CPU to another during its lifetime.

process identification number (PID). A number that uniquely identifies a process.

semaphore. A shared data structure used to synchronize the actions of multiple cooperating processes.

shared data. Data that is accessible by more than one process.

static scheduling. A scheduling method that assigns tasks to processes at run time in a pre-determined fashion. For example, a statically scheduled data-partitioning program might divide loop iterations evenly among processes.

System V Applications Environment. A collection of utilities, libraries, man pages, and other files which, when installed, provide an environment that is nearly identical to that of UNIX System V. Refer to the *DYNIX SVAE Summary* for more information.

Index

About Sequent

Founded in 1983, Sequent Computer Systems is located near Portland, Oregon. Sequent Computer Systems announced the first easy-to-use parallel computer, the Sequent B8000, in September, 1984. Since then, Sequent has established a leadership position in delivering parallel computing products for mainstream applications. The Sequent B21000 was introduced in January, 1986, extending the performance of Sequent's fully compatible, scalable systems into the mainframe range. In May, 1987, Sequent announced the Symmetry Series S27 and S81 systems. The Symmetry Series is based on the existing Sequent system architecture and is source-compatible with the Balance Series, but its higher-speed CPUs extend the Sequent systems performance range to 81 MIPs.

Sequent systems combine the ease-of-use of the standard UNIX® operating system with the performance advantages of multiple tightly-coupled 32-bit microprocessors, each offering supermini performance. DYNIX®, Sequent's implementation of the UNIX operating system, can execute both 4.2bsd and System V applications simultaneously. In multiuser applications, DYNIX makes the parallel architecture completely transparent to existing user software, automatically balancing process loads across the multiple processors. Sequent systems also provide facilities for explicit large- and small-grain parallel programming. FORTRAN, C, Pascal, and Ada® compilers, programming aids, communications software, and PC interface software are available. Sequent's extensive third party software referral program and catalog, "LINKS", includes the leading relational data base management systems, office automation software, cross-development tools, numerous spreadsheet programs and a variety of other utilities.

Other Sequent publications for programmers:

DYNIX Programmer's Manual Volumes I and II

Sequent C Compiler User's Manual

Sequent FORTRAN Compiler User's Manual

Sequent Pascal Compiler User's Manual

Balance Series Assembler User's Manual

Symmetry Series Assembler User's Manual

Sequent Pdbx User's Manual

Pdbx Quick Reference